TASTE OF AUSTRALIA

Lyndey Milan

CONTENTS

INTRODUCTION

This book is the culmination of over 12 months' filming to make the 14-part TV series *Lyndey Milan's Taste of Australia*. But it is also much, much more. Dip inside to find the heart and soul of modern Australia. Meet the characters who grow clean, green world-class produce, and the cooks and chefs who transform it, and delight in the vibrant, multicultural, irreverent personality that is Australian food and wine.

Australia is a country full of surprises and contrasts, famous for its beaches and wildlife. Yet it also has ever-evolving food and wine industries, which can take their place with the best in the world. This is what I uncovered during filming and celebrate in this book.

Before settlement by the First Fleet in 1788 there was, of course, an Australian Indigenous cuisine based on native flora and fauna. However, the first white settlers preferred to adapt the old customs and traditions of Europe. Available ingredients were substituted, and so improvisation and experimentation became part of Australia's cooking culture. With successive waves of migrants, first from post-war Europe and later from Asia, even more new foods and techniques were adopted.

Australians are great travellers and happily brought home foreign tastes and flavours. Australian food and wine writers brought back tales and recipes that we shared. Australian chefs also travelled. With no distinct Australian cuisine, new ideas were easily incorporated into our food style, first by our chefs but increasingly these ideas trickled down to the every day. There were never any restrictive written rules or traditions, such as were found in Europe, advising the correct way to cook or which grapes could be planted, when they could be picked and how they could be treated. So there has always been a freedom around food and wine that has also been fed by an amazing availability of fresh produce from both the sea and the land.

Australia is such a huge continent that it has every growing condition from sub-tropical to cool, from maritime to inland. There are few ingredients, even unusual ones, that won't grow somewhere in this country. Eclecticism rules and so, when I was further developing recipes for this book beyond those in the show, I was able to celebrate the flavours of the world; from South America to Scandinavia, from Europe to Asia – not forgetting our own native Australian flavours.

TOP: Lyndey at Goldfields Honey,
Castlemaine, Victoria.

BOTTOM LEFT: Lyndey and chocolate maker
Josh Bahen, of Bahen & Co., Margaret River,
Western Australia.

BOTTOM RIGHT: Lyndey in the herb garden
at Canberra's Floriade.

PAGE 4: Lyndey preparing to cook Pork steaks with
nettle sauce, pickle, asparagus and broad bean salad
(recipe page 81) at Cullen Wines, Margaret River,
Western Australia.

I was brought up to be a proud Australian – and to be thankful for and respectful of my homeland. My mum was a good home cook and she and Dad had a knack for entertaining. They lived and breathed the hospitality of the table. This was to become my mantra and one I shared with my children, Lucy and Blair, as they grew up.

Having made TV series in other countries – *Lyndey & Blair's Taste of Greece* and *Lyndey Milan's Taste of Ireland* – it was inconceivable that Australia would not be the next country to get the 'Taste of' treatment. So, with camera crew in tow, I was on a mission; rolling up my sleeves and pulling on my gumboots to get to the heart of Australia.

During my travels I climbed the Sydney Harbour Bridge, travelled to the cobbled lanes of Melbourne's caffeine-enriched foodie mecca and explored vineyards small and large and the rolling hills and lush greenery of the hinterland. From the crystal-clear oceans that define our coastline to the raw and unforgiving earth of the outback, I travelled to the bush to meet the farmers and the characters who are the backbone of Australia. Everything was on the menu and nothing was off limits as I explored the real 'Taste of Australia'. I spent more than 12 months wading through rivers and paddocks, cooking fabulous food among cows, pigs and goats, in temperatures from 2°C (35°F) to over 40°C (104°F). It was a bit like a 'girls' own' adventure as I fed kangaroos on Pebbly Beach, rode a camel on the beach in Port Macquarie, went fly fishing in Canberra, dragon boat racing on Lake Burley Griffin, flew across the tulips at Floriade on a crane, rode a trike in the Barossa, milked a goat, rode a brumby and fished for Murray cod in the Snowy Mountains, went boot scootin' at Tamworth, was surrounded by dolphins at Huskisson, panned for gold in the middle of winter in Orange, chopped wood at the Sydney Royal Easter Show, took a balloon ride at sunrise in Canowindra, learnt beekeeping at Goldfields Inn and wrapped it all up with a canoe ride at sunset on the Margaret River in Western Australia.

This book showcases the bountiful variety of food and wine from the many landscapes I visited: the city, the vines, the waterways, the bush and the high country. Australia is a gastronomic delight; all brought to life by the unique characters who help reveal our thriving Australian culinary culture. I hope you enjoy my Taste of Australia.

Lyndey Milan

THE
CITY

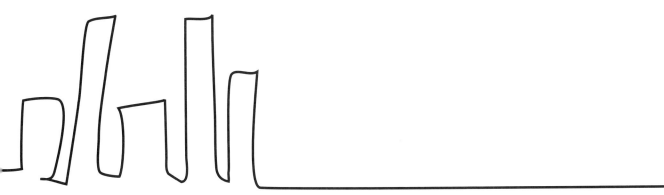

Sydney is Australia's biggest city with a population of just under 5 million. It's my
hometown and holds a special place in my heart. There's no better place to be
introduced to this city than on the Sydney Harbour BridgeClimb with its incomparable
view of the Opera House, the city, the coastline, the harbour and the network of
waterways going inland. Completed in 1932 the bridge is still the largest single-span
arch bridge in the world.

There are any number of beaches, parks and public spaces in Sydney, ideal for picnics
or for cooking with one of the most dynamic chefs in the world, Neil Perry. With seven
restaurants – in Sydney, Melbourne and Perth – it made a pleasant change to get him
out of the kitchen and down by the harbour. Neil is especially proud of his long-term
consultancy with the Australian flagship airline Qantas on their food offering for both
their inflight and lounge menus. As Neil says, 'Qantas is a major buyer of Australian raw
ingredients ... for wine, it's the third-biggest purchaser behind the two supermarkets. But
we're a shop window – we're serving it to people and letting people see great Australian
wine brands. It's so important to small food producers and wine producers.'

Neil works closely with suppliers like Vic's Meat, which also has an amazing retail shop
in Woollahra, where consumers can experience the same high-quality product. Dating
from 1876, this is the oldest continually run butcher shop in Australia. Victor Churchill,
named in honour of the founding Churchill family and master butcher Victor Puharich,
is now run with Vic's son Anthony, a fifth-generation butcher. Its breathtaking design pays
homage to traditional Parisian butcher shops but with a glass-fronted ageing room with
Himalayan rock salt walls, a revolving rack of meat, butchers working on handcrafted
timber butchers' blocks, mosaic-like marble tiles and cow-hide walls. Suppliers like these

work closely with both the chefs and their own suppliers, the farmers, always striving for sustainable, ethical and great tasting product. The shop is also a charcuterie and traiteur, complete with rotisserie, which gives off the enticing aroma of roast chicken. Anthony himself has become quite a star with his own TV series and popular app, *Ask the Butcher*.

When most of us are still tucked up in bed, Sydney's Flemington wholesale markets, the horticultural gateway to Australia, is a hive of activity. Every night 500 trucks and forklifts haul in a stack of fruit, vegetables and flowers with the voices of traders bargaining and bantering. It's a massive operation and equates to 2.2 million tonnes (2.4 million tons) to feed nearly a third of Australia. Its sister retail market, Paddy's Markets, in the heart of Chinatown, has its own specialties to offer. My dear friend Jennice Kersh first visited these markets in a pram with her mother Edna, after whom she and her brother Ray named their restaurant and now their catering business, Edna's Table. Jennice believes the heart and soul of any city is its market and she showed me her favourite stalls.

I'm more at home with food than the catwalk, but Mercedes-Benz Fashion Week Australia is always fun and, like anything, inevitably involves food and wine. A fabulous design duo making waves, Aje, are sponsored by hip wine label Tempus Two, so an after-show dinner gives me a chance to meet the designers – and comment on the food and wine matching.

Every year the country comes to the city at the Sydney Royal Easter Show, Australia's largest event, which attracts around 900,000 visitors each year. This 14-day extravaganza celebrates excellence in Australian agriculture via competition, display and education. Sure, there is a fun fair element and showbags too but, for me, the highlights are always the wood-chopping, the District Exhibits of 50,000 pieces of fresh produce from different competing areas of New South Wales and southeast Queensland, and the Grand Parade in the main arena – the largest choreographed animal parade in the world, showcasing prize-winning cattle, horses, dogs, sheep, goats and pigs. I am very proud to be the first female Vice-President of the Royal Agricultural Society of New South Wales, which runs this amazing event, and was thrilled to bring it to life on screen, wood-chopping with 1000-time world champion David Foster, learning the secrets of the Country Women's Association scones and participating in the pumpkin bowling under the District Exhibits.

TOP: Lyndey jamming with the Stiletto Sisters, some of Melbourne's laneway entertainers.

BOTTOM LEFT: Vittoria Coffee College teaches the fine art of making espresso.

BOTTOM RIGHT: Lyndey with Sisto Malaspina, owner of Melbourne's Pellegrini's Cafe.

Australia also has a world-class coffee culture, thanks to successive waves of Italian migrants, especially after the Second World War. Vittoria imported a coffee-roasting machine as early as 1958 to roast coffee, fresh in Australia. However, Melbourne, Australia's second-largest city, is the coffee capital. Here Italians opened cafés in the '50s, with one of the earliest being Pellegrini's, which opened in 1954. With Italian accents and food, it still feels like a little part of Italy. Alternatively, the Melbourne laneways, with the coming together of music, art, eclectic shops, coffee and friends, create vibrant meeting places.

Melbourne takes its food pretty seriously, too, and one of its home-grown heroes is celebrity chef Pete Evans. While we worked together as co-hosts of the TV show *Fresh* on the 9 Network for several years, his move to Channel 7 and *My Kitchen Rules* has launched him into the stratosphere. As a regular visitor to the US, he has appeared on *The Martha Stewart Show* and cooked for the gang at NBC's *Today* show. But he is never one to forget old mates and his philosophy is to cook with love and laughter. Recently he's become an ambassador for the Australian Organic Schools Program and suggested we hook up at the Sophia Mundi Steiner School in suburban Abbotsford. Here the kids care for the garden and learn how to grow, harvest and cook organic vegies. Their joyful voices and enthusiasm show how much they thrive on this. The kids were enthralled, too, to watch me learn about a completely different, organic, way of growing things.

Adelaide is the charming capital of South Australia, with a population of just over a million. Much as it is the gateway to some of Australia's most accessible wine regions, it is also home to a very different type of agriculture. Nick Femia, from South Australian Mushrooms, showed me the light by taking me into the dark, behind the scenes at his farm in Waterloo Corner. What an incredible sight were the sprawling rows of white buttons, Swiss browns and portobellos growing on racks in sheds! Once the mushroom spore grows through the pasteurised compost, the mushrooms grow at an amazing millimetre (³⁄₆₄ in) an hour, doubling every 24 hours. Although there are no weather challenges, the growing rooms need to be constantly monitored for temperature, compost temperature, relative humidity and the CO_2. Nick's enthusiasm and passion for these fleshy fungi is contagious and a highlight of my visit was again with children, seeing the looks on the faces as a regular tour for schoolkids came through.

I will never forget my first taste of almond gazpacho – I was entranced by the flavour and texture. I first created this recipe to be served in a shot glass for my TV special, Lyndey's Cracking Christmas, but it translates beautifully into an appetiser.

ALMOND GAZPACHO WITH SEARED SCALLOPS AND PARSLEY OIL

SERVES 4 as an appetiser

PREPARATION 10 minutes, plus 1 hour (or overnight) refrigeration

COOKING 3 minutes

220 g (8 oz) white sourdough bread, crusts removed, cut into cubes
155 g (5½ oz/1 cup) blanched almonds
2 garlic cloves, peeled
1 teaspoon sea salt flakes
60 ml (2 fl oz/¼ cup) sherry vinegar, or to taste
125 ml (4 fl oz/½ cup) extra-virgin olive oil, plus 1 tablespoon extra for frying

salt and freshly ground black pepper
12 scallops (about 240 g/8½ oz), without roe

PARSLEY OIL
30 g (1 oz/½ cup) flat-leaf (Italian) parsley leaves
60 ml (2 fl oz/¼ cup) extra-virgin olive oil

WINE

Sherry is a classic match for soup, especially one like this that is Spanish-inspired. Note that Australian sherry is now known as apera.

LYNDEY'S NOTE

In Australia sea scallops have the orange roe on them. Saucer scallops are usually sold roe-off and on the shell. It's really up to you which you use.

For the parsley oil, bring a small saucepan of water to the boil. Add the parsley leaves and boil for 15 seconds. Drain and refresh under cold running water. Squeeze the parsley leaves dry using paper towel. In a food processor, blend the parsley leaves and oil until smooth. Drain through a fine sieve and discard the parsley pulp.

Soak the bread briefly in 500 ml (17 fl oz/2 cups) water. Using a blender, finely chop the almonds, garlic and sea salt flakes. Add the bread with the soaking water and blend to a smooth paste. With the motor running, add the sherry vinegar and the 125 ml (4 fl oz/½ cup) oil in a thin, steady stream. Season to taste with salt and pepper. Refrigerate for at least an hour before serving. (This can be made up to a day ahead.)

To serve, heat the extra tablespoon of oil in a small frying pan over high heat. Season the scallops with salt and pepper. Cook the scallops for 1 minute each side or until caramelised and just opaque.

Pour the chilled gazpacho into soup bowls and top with the scallops and a drizzle of parsley oil.

Also known as Roman egg drop soup, celebrity chef Pete Evans cooked this with me in the grounds of the Sophia Mundi Steiner School with silverbeet (Swiss chard), parsley and kale grown by the kids. Pete is an ambassador for the Australian Organic Schools Program.

STRACCIATELLA SOUP WITH CAVOLO NERO

SERVES 4

PREPARATION
10 minutes

COOKING
15 minutes

WINE

This soup has both flavour and texture, but if you top it with the spicy kale chips, care needs to be taken with the cayenne pepper heat, so try a pinot gris or marsanne.

1 litre (34 fl oz/4 cups) chicken stock
100 g (3½ oz) cavolo nero (Tuscan cabbage), silverbeet (Swiss chard) or English spinach, roughly chopped
4 free-range eggs
⅓ cup chopped flat-leaf (Italian) parsley

75 g (2¾ oz/¾ cup) freshly grated parmesan
2 teaspoons lemon juice
salt and freshly ground black pepper
12 thin slices lardo (cured pork fat) or extra-virgin olive oil to drizzle (optional)

Bring the chicken stock to the boil in a saucepan. Add the cavolo nero to the stock and wilt for 1–2 minutes.

Beat the eggs, parsley, parmesan and lemon juice together with a fork and season with salt and pepper. Pour into the stock and stir for 1 minute with a large spoon.

Serve topped with the lardo or oil. Add Crisp kale chips (page 37) if desired.

Sydney rock is the name of a variety of oyster, and doesn't refer to where they are grown. But in a chapter entitled 'The City', I couldn't go past a recipe using them, though Pacific oysters work equally well. As a nod to the craze for all things Mexican, I have used an authentic salsa. Pico de gallo is a fresh, uncooked salsa.

OYSTERS WITH PICO DE GALLO

MAKES 24

PREPARATION
10 minutes

WINE
The salsa in this recipe has acid from the lime juice and tomatoes and a kick from the chilli, so a sauvignon blanc or riesling would be the best match.

2 small roma (plum) tomatoes, peeled, seeded and diced
1 small red onion, finely chopped
1 green jalapeño chilli, seeded and finely chopped
zest and juice of 1 lime
1/3 cup finely chopped coriander (cilantro) leaves
sea salt flakes
24 freshly shucked oysters on the shell

Combine the tomato, onion, jalapeño, lime zest and juice, coriander and salt to taste; mix well. Spoon over the oysters and serve.

Churrasco is a Brazilian word meaning 'barbecued' or 'grilled on skewers'. Although often served with chimichurri sauce – a lovely herby sauce with garlic, oregano and red wine vinegar – I've chosen the lesser known aji sauce from Peru – a sweet onion and jalapeño combination that is a little like a South American version of Thai nam jim dipping sauce. It also goes well with empanadas, grilled meats and seafood.

CHURRASCO PRAWNS WITH AJI SAUCE

SERVES 8 as a canapé or 4 as an appetiser

PREPARATION 15 minutes

COOKING 5 minutes

WINE

White wine lovers can try sauvignon blanc, but for red wine try a malbec, the premium grape variety of South America.

1 kg (2 lb 3 oz) large raw prawns (shrimp), peeled and deveined, heads removed, tails intact
wooden skewers, soaked in cold water or placed in the freezer for 30 minutes
extra-virgin olive oil for brushing

AJI SAUCE
4 green jalapeño chillies, seeded
3 spring onions (scallions), roughly sliced
¼ cup roughly chopped coriander (cilantro) stems and leaves
2 tablespoons red wine vinegar
½ teaspoon grated lime zest
2 teaspoons lime juice
2 teaspoons extra-virgin olive oil
salt and freshly ground black pepper

For the aji sauce, place the jalapeños, spring onion and coriander in a small food processor and process until finely chopped. Add the red wine vinegar, lime zest and juice and oil and continue to process until smooth. Season with salt and pepper.

Preheat a barbecue or chargrill pan to high.

For the prawns, insert a wooden skewer at the tail and push through the length of the prawn. Brush the prawns with oil and cook on the barbecue or in the chargrill pan for 2 minutes each side or until cooked through. Serve with the aji sauce.

The flamboyant Jennice Kersh and her brother Raymond ran the legendary Edna's Table Restaurant in Sydney for over 25 years. They were the true pioneers of Australian native foods. Ray, who trained as a theatrical costumier, has a way with presentation, but also has a knack for weaving Indigenous flavours in with other foods.

CROCODILE NORI TEMPURA CIGAR

MAKES 12 canapés

PREPARATION
20 minutes

COOKING
20 minutes

WINE

Look for a sparkling wine, but as Ray's food is always bursting with flavour, try a sparkling rosé rather than a white.

LYNDEY'S NOTE

Test if the oil is hot enough by dipping a wooden spoon handle in – if it bubbles it is hot!

1 tablespoon extra-virgin olive oil
2 cm (¾ in) piece fresh ginger, finely chopped
2 garlic cloves, finely chopped
½ leek, thinly sliced
1 small corn cob
1 small zucchini (courgette), sliced into thin matchsticks
1 tablespoon finely chopped basil
250 g (9 oz) minced (ground) crocodile (or chicken and pork mince)
salt and freshly ground black pepper

3 sheets nori
12 wonton skins
1 egg, beaten
oil for deep-frying

TEMPURA BATTER
75 g (2¾ oz/½ cup) cornflour (cornstarch)
75 g (2¾ oz/½ cup) plain (all-purpose) flour
125 ml (4 fl oz/½ cup) chilled soda water (club soda), plus extra if needed
70 g (2½ oz/½ cup) ice cubes

Heat the tablespoon extra-virgin olive oil in a saucepan over medium heat. Add the ginger, garlic and leek and cook for 5 minutes or until softened. Set aside to cool.

Slice the kernels from the corn cob and add to the cooled leek mixture with the zucchini, basil and minced crocodile. Season to taste with salt and pepper and mix well.

Cut each nori sheet into four even squares. Cut the wonton skins diagonally, just off the corner so that there are three long sides and one very short side. Lay a nori square flat. Brush two adjacent sides with egg. Stick a wonton half, along its longest diagonal side, to one end of the nori square. Stick another wonton half along the adjacent side of the nori square in the same way. Repeat with the remaining nori squares and wonton halves.

Roll a heaped tablespoon of the crocodile mixture into a finger-shape and place along one of the wonton halves. Fold over the short overlapping piece of wonton so the filling can't come out. Egg wash the opposite top half of the nori square. Roll up the wonton to encase the filling completely. You will end up with a cigar shape with the nori on the outside and the other wonton flaring out the top. Twist this end of the parcel to look like a bonbon parcel. Repeat with the remaining nori squares, wonton sheets and crocodile mixture.

For the tempura batter, mix the ingredients roughly in a large bowl (ideally it should be a little lumpy). Add more soda water if you need to lighten the batter.

Place a large saucepan or deep-fryer of oil over high heat until hot. Deep-fry the parcels, in batches, for approximately 5–7 minutes until golden brown. Drain on paper towel and serve while hot.

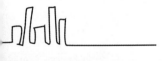

Australia began farming Atlantic salmon in Tasmania in the early 1980s, giving many people their first chance to try this fantastic fish. Our nearby cousins in New Zealand grow a different species of salmon called king salmon (originally chinook), which is also grown in pristine cool waters. Both types are popular in restaurants but can be so easily prepared at home.

QUICK-CURED SALMON WITH JAPANESE SOBA NOODLE SALAD

SERVES 4

PREPARATION
15 minutes, plus
1 hour curing

COOKING
15 minutes

WINE
The rich, luscious flavours of salmon respond well to an elegant, cool-climate chardonnay, which can also handle the Asian flavours. Alternatively you could try a rosé.

125 g (4¹/₂ oz) soba noodles
1 tablespoon extra-virgin olive oil
3 spring onions (scallions), sliced diagonally
150 g (5¹/₂ oz) mixed mushrooms (oyster, enoki, shimeji etc.), thinly sliced if necessary
100 g (3¹/₂ oz) snow peas (mangetout), thickly sliced
1 tablespoon sake (optional)
¹/₄ cup basil leaves
¹/₄ cup coriander (cilantro) leaves

QUICK-CURED SALMON
1 tablespoon caster (superfine) sugar
3 teaspoons sea salt flakes
200 g (7 oz) salmon, pin-boned and skinned

JAPANESE DRESSING
1 teaspoon wasabi paste
2 tablespoons sliced pickled ginger
1 garlic clove, finely chopped
2 tablespoons ponzu sauce
1 teaspoon sesame oil

For the quick-cured salmon, combine the sugar and salt in a medium bowl, add the salmon and gently toss until well coated. Cover with plastic wrap, weight down (a plate topped with tins or jars works well) and set aside for 1 hour. Drain well, brushing off the excess salt, and slice thinly.

While the salmon is curing, cook the soba noodles in boiling salted water according to the packet instructions until just tender. Drain well and rinse with cold water.

Combine the Japanese dressing ingredients in a small bowl, mix well and set aside.

Heat the olive oil in a large frying pan over high heat and sauté the spring onions, mushrooms and snow peas for 2 minutes or until starting to soften. Add the soba noodles and Japanese dressing and toss over high heat for 2 minutes until the noodles are warm.

Serve the salmon on a bed of noodles, sprinkled with sake, if using, torn basil and coriander leaves.

Chef Neil Perry is a fan of Rangers Valley beef, supplied by Vic's Meat in Woollahra, Sydney. This was his choice for a harbour-front barbecue with the Opera House and Sydney Harbour Bridge as a backdrop.

BARBECUED BEEF RUMP WITH GARLIC AND PARSLEY DRESSING AND GRILLED SALAD

SERVES 4

PREPARATION
10 minutes

COOKING
10 minutes,
plus resting

WINE
One of Australia's gifts to the wine world has been the blending of cabernet and shiraz, so why not try one of those here?

4 x 250 g (9 oz) sirloin steaks
extra-virgin olive oil for brushing
sea salt
shaved parmesan to serve (optional)

GRILLED SALAD
3 zucchini (courgettes), sliced into
   5 mm x 7 cm (¼ in x 2¾ in) strips
2 eggplants (aubergines), cut into
   1 cm (½ in) slices
4 large tomatoes, cored and quartered
1 tablespoon extra-virgin olive oil
sea salt to taste

1 tablespoon balsamic vinegar
freshly ground black pepper
1 tablespoon flat-leaf (Italian) parsley

GARLIC AND PARSLEY DRESSING
sea salt to taste
2 garlic cloves
3 tablespoons chopped flat-leaf (Italian)
   parsley
2 tablespoons extra-virgin olive oil
freshly ground black pepper
juice of 1 lemon

Remove the steaks from the refrigerator 2 hours before you intend to start cooking. Preheat the barbecue to hot. (This could take up to 1 hour if using natural fuel or 15 minutes for a gas barbecue.) Ensure the grill bars are clean.

Brush the steaks with oil and season liberally with sea salt just before placing on the grill at a 45 degree angle to the grill bars. Cook for a few minutes each side. When halfway through cooking the first side, turn the steaks 45 degrees in the opposite direction to make nice criss-cross grill marks. When done, turn them over and cook the other side. Put the steaks on a plate, cover with foil and place near the barbecue to keep warm. Rest for 10 minutes.

For the grilled salad, make sure the grill bars are hot and clean. Brush the zucchini, eggplant and tomato with a little oil and sprinkle with sea salt. Chargrill the vegetables on both sides until tender. Combine the vegetables in a bowl, add the balsamic vinegar, pepper and the tablespoon of oil and combine. Cool, then add the parsley and check the seasoning.

For the garlic and parsley dressing, on a chopping board with a little sea salt, crush the garlic, add the parsley and chop until you have a paste. Place in a bowl and add the oil, season with pepper, squeeze in the lemon juice and mix to combine. To serve, slice the rested steak with the grilled salad. Drizzle with the garlic and parsley dressing and top with parmesan shavings, if desired.

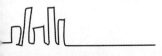

Every Aussie loves a barbie. With this clever combination you can please carnivores and vegetarians alike. First, speak extremely firmly to your butcher and insist that you want very, very thinly sliced and untrimmed beef brisket. He will think you are mad, as usually brisket is braised long and slow. However, in this recipe, flash-cooking keeps the meat tender.

BARBECUED BEEF BRISKET WITH TOFU AND PEANUT SAMBAL

SERVES 4

PREPARATION 20 minutes, plus 30 minutes marinating

COOKING 8 minutes

WINE
This dish has some powerful flavours so it can stand up to a durif or zinfandel.

LYNDEY'S NOTE
If desired, increase the marinade quantities and marinate the tofu for 30 minutes, too, to give it a richer flavour.

500 g (1 lb 2 oz) beef brisket, untrimmed, thinly sliced into 3 mm (¼ in) slices
300 g (10½ oz) firm tofu, cut into twelve 1 cm (½ in) slices
rice flour to dust tofu
1 bunch bulb spring onions (scallions), leaves on, halved
extra-virgin olive oil to brush the tofu and spring onions
1 large butter lettuce, leaves separated

MARINADE
2.5 cm (1 in) piece fresh ginger, peeled and grated
2 garlic cloves, finely chopped
3 tablespoons brown sugar
60 ml (2 fl oz/¼ cup) soy sauce
2 tablespoons Chinese rice wine
2 tablespoons sesame oil
¼ teaspoon freshly ground black pepper

PEANUT SAMBAL
120 g (4½ oz/¾ cup) roasted peanuts
2 garlic cloves, chopped
2 large red chillies, seeded and roughly chopped
2 eschalots, peeled and roughly chopped
¼ cup coriander (cilantro) leaves and roots
1 tablespoon brown sugar
125 ml (4 fl oz/½ cup) lime juice (about 3 limes)
1 tablespoon fish sauce

Combine the marinade ingredients in a flat, non-reactive dish. Add the beef and marinate for 30 minutes. While the beef is marinating make the peanut sauce by either pounding the peanuts, garlic, chillies, eschalots and coriander together using a mortar and pestle or a small food processor, until ground but chunky. Mix through the brown sugar, lime juice and fish sauce. Spoon into a serving bowl and set aside.

Dry the tofu slices with paper towel and toss in the rice flour.

Preheat the barbecue to searingly hot. Brush the spring onions with oil and chargrill on the flat plate of the barbecue with the tofu slices for 3 minutes on each side, until the spring onions are charred and the tofu slices are golden. Remove. Drain the beef well, pat dry on paper towel and flash-cook on the grill of the barbecue for a minute or so on each side, to sear, but do not cook through or the beef will toughen. Serve as an 'assemble your own' dish – brisket, spring onions and tofu with the sambal and lettuce leaves.

Anthony Puharich from Victor Churchill butcher says, 'I love to cook lamb. This preparation requires a little extra from your butcher but will reward with a deep flavour and a great contrast in the meat.' It is 'Roman' as it is named after abbacchio alla romana, an Easter treat celebrated all over Rome. Traditionally it is whole baby lamb simply flavoured with rosemary and olive oil and eaten in its entirety, with nothing wasted. So this recipe of Anthony's makes use of the whole rib.

ROMAN LAMB AND GREEN BEANS WITH ANCHOVY

SERVES 4

PREPARATION
15 minutes, plus
4 hours marinating

COOKING
45 minutes,
plus resting

LYNDEY'S NOTE

Leaving the bone untrimmed gives lovely long bones. You could use normal racks of lamb, but preferably not French-trimmed.

2 x 8 rib racks of lamb with the breast (or belly) still attached, bones untrimmed
2 garlic bulbs, peeled and smashed
1 large bunch rosemary
1 teaspoon sea salt
100 ml (3½ fl oz) extra-virgin olive oil
400 g (14 oz) trimmed green beans

1 tablespoon sherry vinegar or red wine vinegar
1 tablespoon dijon mustard
pinch of sugar
salt and freshly ground black pepper
6 anchovy fillets, halved

Ask your butcher for 8 rib racks of lamb with the breast (or belly) still attached and the fat cap on. Trim some of the skin and stamp, leaving a thin layer of fat. Remove the feather-bone at the shoulder end of the rack. Leave the chine bone (the spine) in place, but ask your butcher to mark the joints with a bandsaw at thick intervals, e.g. between every second cutlet. The cut should be deep enough so you can cut through the bone after cooking. This gives a lovely, large plate of lamb and a beautiful combination of the lean meat from the loin and the richer, unctuous meat from the intercostals (between the ribs) and the belly of the lamb.

Marinate the lamb in the garlic, rosemary, sea salt and half the oil overnight if possible (but for at least 4 hours).

»»»

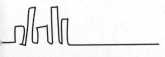

WINE

Although many say shiraz is the natural accompaniment to lamb, I am a fan of cabernet and cabernet blends with it. However, this lamb would go with either. Or as this dish is Italian-style, try a sangiovese.

Heat a barbecue to high 20 minutes before cooking and, when ready to cook, turn down by a third. Place the lamb on the barbecue, fat side down first. Close the hood, but keep a close eye on it, checking the lamb every 5 minutes or so. Closing the hood will add a smoky flavour to the lamb, but do keep in mind that this is not a roasting recipe. You should open the hood around the halfway mark.

You need to get a nice level of colour and caramelisation on the fat of the meat. Cooking fat side down first will give you time to let the fat render, and will protect the lean eye of meat, but do flip it towards the end to ensure you get a nice brown colour on both sides.

Once the lamb is cooked (around 25–30 minutes), remove from the barbecue and allow to rest for around half the cooking time.

Steam or boil the beans for 4–5 minutes or until just tender. Drain and cool under running cold or iced water. Pat dry with paper towel.

Whisk together the vinegar, mustard, sugar, remaining oil and a little salt and pepper in a small bowl. Place the beans onto a large platter. Top with the anchovy halves. Drizzle over the dressing and add some freshly ground black pepper.

Cut long cutlets, using the cuts made by your butcher in the chine bone as a guide. You will end up with lovely Roman-style cutlets, then serve with the rosemary and some of the smashed garlic on the side.

Celebrity chef Neil Perry loves to cook at home for his family and shared this recipe with me. Lamb, mint and peas is a classic combination, beloved by Australians. For a more traditional take, serve it with mashed potato (page 152) or, in trendy city mode, the Cauliflower 'couscous' (page 37).

LAMB, MINT AND PEA PIE

SERVES 4

PREPARATION
20 minutes

COOKING 2½ hours

WINE

Lamb, especially with a fresh herb like mint, is well matched to cabernet sauvignon or a blend of this. Sometimes the grapes pick up a slight eucalypt character from gum trees around the vines.

1 kg (2 lb 3 oz) lamb shoulder, trimmed and cut into 2 cm (¾ in) dice
salt and freshly ground black pepper
2 tablespoons plain (all-purpose) flour
80 ml (2½ fl oz/⅓ cup) extra-virgin olive oil
1 large brown onion, finely diced
2½ tablespoons tomato paste (concentrated purée)
190 ml (6½ fl oz/¾ cup) red wine
190 ml (6½ fl oz/¾ cup) veal stock
180 g (6½ oz/1½ cups) frozen green peas
1 handful of mint leaves, chopped
1 sheet frozen butter puff pastry
1 egg yolk, lightly whisked

Preheat the oven to 150°C (300°F).

Season the lamb with salt and pepper and toss with 1 tablespoon of the flour until evenly coated. Heat the oil in a large, ovenproof heavy-based saucepan or flameproof casserole over high heat. Add the lamb in batches and cook for 1–2 minutes, or until well browned, then remove from the pan.

Add the onion with a pinch of salt and cook over low heat for 5 minutes, or until softened. Add the tomato paste and the remaining flour and cook for a minute or so. Add the red wine and veal stock and stir until the mixture boils. Return the lamb to the pan, cover and place in the oven for 2 hours, or until the lamb is tender. Stir through the peas and mint. Season to taste with salt and pepper.

Increase the oven temperature to 200°C (400°F). Divide the pie filling among four 250 ml (8½ fl oz/1 cup) ramekins or pie dishes.

Remove the pastry from the freezer only 5–10 minutes before needed, so it thaws but stays chilled. Cut the pastry into four. Top each pie with a piece of pastry – it should be large enough to hang over the edge of each dish. Press the pastry down firmly around the edges of the dishes and brush evenly with the egg yolk. Bake in the middle of the oven for about 15 minutes, or until puffed and golden. Serve warm.

Paola Cocchis and Luisa Lacota, the 'Italian mammas', started the school canteen at the Sophia Mundi Steiner School in Melbourne to provide fresh healthy organic meals for all the children in the school community. They shared this recipe with me. The vegetables make a pesto-like sauce.

HIDDEN VEG PESTO PASTA

SERVES 4

PREPARATION
10 minutes

COOKING
15 minutes

WINE

For the adults only try a viognier, which has a natural affinity with vegetables

LYNDEY'S NOTE

Grana Padano is a northern Italian hard cheese, which is subtler, less nutty and cheaper than Parmigiano Reggiano. You can substitute any parmesan. The extra pesto (without the zucchini) can be frozen in ice cube trays or small containers.

salt to taste
500 g (1 lb 2 oz) green vegetables (zucchini/courgette, English spinach, broccoli)
400 g (14 oz) spelt or kamut pasta
2 bunches (250 g/9 oz) basil, washed and dried

1 garlic clove
50 g (1¾ oz/⅔ cup) freshly grated Grana Padano, plus extra shaved to serve
60 ml (2 fl oz/¼ cup) extra-virgin olive oil
1 tablespoon lemon juice

Bring a large saucepan of salted water to the boil. Add the greens and boil until soft, about 2–3 minutes. Remove with a slotted spoon and allow to cool. Throw your pasta into the pan and cook as per the instructions on the packet.

While your pasta is cooking, pick the basil leaves off the stems and place in a food processor along with the garlic, cheese and 1 tablespoon of the oil. Process the ingredients and slowly add the remaining oil until you have a smooth, thick paste. You may need to scrape down the side and process a little longer as the occasional leaf may climb the side of the bowl. Once you have a nice smooth consistency, remove the pesto from the bowl leaving behind about 125 g (4½ oz/½ cup) in the food processor. Add the greens to the food processor, salt to taste, add the lemon juice then process again.

Strain your pasta, reserving 125 ml (4 fl oz/½ cup) of the pasta water. Toss the pasta through the sauce, moisten with pasta water, if desired, and serve immediately with the extra cheese.

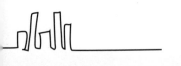

Celebrity chef Pete Evans loves good, natural food. He rates these kale chips as a healthier alternative to potato crisps. They certainly are moreish! Adjust the cayenne pepper to suit your own taste.

CRISP KALE CHIPS

SERVES 8–10

PREPARATION
10 minutes

COOKING
15 minutes

TO DRINK
Why not try a beer with these?

1 large bunch kale or cavolo nero (Tuscan cabbage)
60 ml (2 fl oz/¼ cup) extra-virgin olive oil or coconut oil

1 teaspoon cayenne pepper, or to taste
sea salt or Himalayan salt and freshly ground black pepper

Preheat the oven to 160°C (320°F).

Wash the kale thoroughly with cold water and then pat dry with paper towel. Remove the kale leaves from the tough ribs and cut the leaves into smaller pieces.

Line a baking tray with baking paper. In a large bowl, toss the kale with the oil, the cayenne pepper and salt and pepper, going easy on the salt as a little will go a long way.

Place the kale on the baking tray in a single layer. Do not overcrowd the tray – use more than one if you need to. Roast the kale until crisp, about 10–15 minutes (check your oven as temperatures may vary).

Serve as a snack or on top of Stracciatella soup with cavolo nero (page 19).

CAULIFLOWER 'COUSCOUS'

SERVES 4 as a side

PREPARATION
10 minutes

COOKING
15 minutes

60 ml (2 fl oz/¼ cup) extra-virgin olive oil
2 large eschalots, finely diced
3 garlic cloves, finely chopped
1 small or ½ large head cauliflower, stalks and stems discarded

salt and freshly ground black pepper
¼ cup chives, roughly chopped
40 g (1½ oz/¼ cup) pine nuts, toasted

Place a frying pan over medium heat and add the oil. Add the eschalots and cook for 2 minutes, then add the garlic and cook until all is soft, approximately 1 more minute.

Chop the cauliflower finely in a food processor and add to the pan with salt and pepper. Cook, stirring frequently, until the cauliflower softens, about 10 minutes. (Add a splash of water if you are afraid it might burn.) Stir through the chives just before serving and sprinkle with the pine nuts.

Another delightful recipe from the Italian mammas, Paola Cocchis and Luisa Lacota, who run the school canteen at the Sophia Mundi Steiner School in Melbourne, providing fresh healthy organic meals for the children. They tell me, 'this is quite a popular dish in the canteen and it's such a joy to see the bowls returned empty [and the children] with happy faces and full tummies!' There's no chilli in this so it is very approachable for anyone. However, feel free to add some chilli if you like!

PUMPKIN, SILVERBEET AND RED LENTIL DAL

SERVES 6–7

PREPARATION
20 minutes

COOKING
30 minutes, plus resting

WINE

Without chilli a viognier will do the trick; with chilli, go for a pinot noir.

2 teaspoons brown mustard seeds
2 teaspoons cumin seeds
2 teaspoons ground turmeric
2 teaspoons garam masala
1 brown onion
1 carrot
3 cm (1¼ in) piece fresh ginger
2 garlic cloves
1 bunch fresh coriander (cilantro)
60 ml (2 fl oz/¼ cup) sunflower oil
150 g (5½ oz) pumpkin (winter squash), cut into 2 cm (¾ in) cubes
250 g (9 oz/1 cup) red lentils

450 g (1 lb/2¼ cups) chopped fresh tomatoes (or one 440 g/15½ oz tin chopped tomatoes)
405 ml (13½ fl oz/1⅔ cups) coconut milk
375 ml (12½ fl oz/1½ cups) water
2 stalks silverbeet (Swiss chard) or English spinach, shredded
juice of 2 limes
thick Greek-style yoghurt to serve (optional)
pappadams to serve (optional)
steamed brown rice to serve (optional)

Grind the mustard and cumin seeds together, using a mortar and pestle or spice grinder, and mix with the other spices. Set aside.

Place the onion, carrot, ginger, garlic and one-third of the bunch of coriander (reserve the rest to chop for garnish) into the food processor and process until very finely chopped, almost paste-like.

Warm the oil in a large frying pan with high sides and add the carrot and onion mix and the spices. Sauté until the spices are aromatic and the mixture is drying a little. Add the pumpkin, lentils, tomatoes, coconut milk and water and bring to a simmer. Cover and stir gently, occasionally, to prevent sticking. Cook for approximately 20 minutes. Stir through the silverbeet and lime juice and cook for another 10 minutes or until the pumpkin and lentils are tender.

To develop the flavours and allow the dal to thicken, let it sit for about 30 minutes before serving.

Serve the dal with a dollop of yoghurt, a crunchy pappadam, a sprinkling of fresh coriander and some steamed brown rice, if desired.

Lemon delicious pudding is a long-time favourite Australian dessert, creating its own gooey sauce. It works just as well with red grapefruit – or any citrus fruit. Strangely, it works exactly the same if you use plain (all-purpose) or self-raising flour, so it doesn't matter which you use.

RED GRAPEFRUIT DELICIOUS PUDDING

SERVES 6

PREPARATION
15 minutes

COOKING
40 minutes

WINE

Moscato is low alcohol and sweet with a slightly frizzante character, which cleanses the palate perfectly for this dish.

LYNDEY'S NOTE

You could make this into six individual desserts by filling six 250 ml (8½ fl oz/1 cup) capacity ovenproof dishes and cook for only 25–30 minutes.

30 g (1 oz) butter, softened
1 teaspoon grated red grapefruit zest
115 g (4 oz/½ cup) caster (superfine) sugar
3 eggs, separated, plus 1 extra egg white

35 g (1¼ oz/¼ cup) flour
125 ml (4 fl oz/½ cup) red grapefruit juice
250 ml (8½ fl oz/1 cup) milk
ice cream or cream to serve (optional)
icing (confectioners') sugar for dusting

Preheat the oven to 180°C (350°F). Grease a deep 1.25 litre (42 fl oz/5 cup) capacity ovenproof dish.

Beat the butter, zest, sugar and egg yolks in a small bowl using an electric mixer until creamy. Beat in the sifted flour and the grapefruit juice then gradually beat in the milk.

Beat the four egg whites in a large clean bowl until firm peaks form. Gently fold through the red grapefruit mixture. Pour the mixture into the prepared dish. Place in a larger baking dish. Pour boiling water into the larger baking dish until halfway up the sides of the smaller dish. Bake for about 40 minutes or until golden brown and just firm to touch. There should be some liquid left in the bottom of the dish, though this will be absorbed if you leave it standing so serve immediately with ice cream or cream, if using, dusted with sifted icing sugar.

When mangoes are out of season, the syrup is delicious with any berries, papaya or even orange segments. Macaroons have long been a favourite sweet treat in Australia, too often superseded by their fancier, French cousin, the macaron.

MANGO WITH GREEN TEA SYRUP, COCONUT CREAM AND MACAROON CRUMBS

SERVES 4

PREPARATION
15 minutes, plus chilling time

COOKING
20 minutes

WINE

It is important to keep the sugar level in a dessert below that in an accompanying wine, so a luscious botrytis semillon is called for here.

LYNDEY'S NOTE

The macaroon recipe makes around 24. This dessert uses half, so store the remainder in an airtight container. If it is a particularly hot day, chill the bowl before whipping the coconut cream.

1 green teabag
1 tablespoon palm sugar (jaggery) or brown sugar
1 teaspoon grated lime zest
1/4 large red chilli, seeded and thinly sliced (optional)
2 mangoes
405 ml (13 1/2 fl oz/1 2/3 cups) coconut cream, chilled overnight
1 teaspoon vanilla bean paste

MACAROONS
1 egg white
115 g (4 oz/1/2 cup) caster (superfine) sugar
1 teaspoon vanilla bean paste
40 g (1 1/2 oz/1/2 cup) shredded coconut

For the macaroons, preheat the oven to 180°C (350°F) and line a baking tray with baking paper. Whisk the egg white using an electric mixer in a medium bowl until soft peaks form. Add the caster sugar, 1 tablespoon at a time, and continue to beat until stiff and glossy. Fold in the vanilla bean paste and shredded coconut. Spoon heaped teaspoons onto the prepared tray and bake for 15 minutes or until just beginning to turn golden on the edges. Cool on a wire rack. Gently peel the macaroons from the baking paper and store in an airtight container until serving.

Combine the green teabag with 125 ml (4 fl oz/1/2 cup) boiling water in a small saucepan and leave to infuse for 5 minutes. Remove the teabag and add the palm sugar, lime zest and chilli, if using. Place over medium heat, bring to the boil and simmer for 5 minutes or until thickened.

Meanwhile cut the cheeks off one of the mangoes, following the line of the stone. Using a large spoon, carefully scoop the flesh away from the skin with a spoon and slice lengthways into 1 cm (1/2 in) slices. Remove the skin from the remaining mango and, using a paring knife, also slice the remaining flesh lengthways into 1 cm (1/2 in) slices. Place the mango slices in a bowl, pour over the syrup, cover and refrigerate until serving. Just before serving pour the well-chilled coconut cream into a large bowl and whip using an electric mixer for 4 minutes or until soft peaks form. Stir through the vanilla bean paste.

To serve, spoon the mango slices and syrup into serving bowls or glasses and top with the whipped coconut cream and some crumbled macaroons.

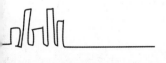

These puddings are a very easy way to achieve what is known as a volcano pudding, with a molten centre. For variation, consider adding a teaspoon of finely grated orange zest or a tablespoon of strong coffee to the pudding mixture. Chilli lovers may like to add a pinch of dried red chilli flakes.

CHOCOLATE HAZELNUT FONDANT PUDDING

SERVES 4

PREPARATION
10 minutes

COOKING
15 minutes

WINE

The strong flavours of chocolate need a rich wine, so try a liqueur muscat or a topaque. If you are using chilli, try a sparkling shiraz.

LYNDEY'S NOTE

Unbaked puddings can be frozen for up to 1 month and chocolate and butter can be melted in the microwave.

30 g (1 oz) butter
200 g (7 oz) dark chocolate
80 g (2¾ oz/⅓ cup) caster (superfine) sugar
2 eggs

1 teaspoon vanilla bean paste
35 g (1¼ oz/⅓ cup) ground hazelnuts
thick (double/heavy) cream or ice cream to serve

Preheat the oven to 180°C (350°F) and grease four 250 ml (8½ fl oz/1 cup) capacity holes in a muffin tin or four ramekins.

Melt the butter and 120 g (4½ oz) of the dark chocolate in a medium saucepan over low heat, stirring to combine. Allow to cool for 2 minutes.

Beat in the caster sugar, eggs and vanilla. Fold in the ground hazelnuts.

Divide the mixture evenly between the four muffin holes. Break the remaining chocolate into four pieces and push a piece of chocolate into the mixture in each muffin hole, smoothing over to ensure that the chocolate is completely covered by the pudding mixture.

Bake for 15 minutes or until just firm to the touch. Allow to cool for 5 minutes before turning out and serving with thick cream or ice cream.

MUSHROOMS

Neither vegetable nor fruit, mushrooms come from the fungi kingdom, with all manner of health benefits. Never wash them; just brush off any dirt, as it is only pasteurised compost and quite safe. There is an increasing variety on the market. The most widely available cultivated mushrooms are white agaricus, including button, cup, flat, Swiss brown and portobello (which are large Swiss browns). Speciality varieties include oyster, enoki, shimeji and king brown. Wild mushrooms are foraged and grow in the colder months and include saffron milk caps also known as pine mushrooms, and slippery Jacks (which are the only mushroom which should be peeled before use).

MUSHROOM IDEAS

Mushrooms are very versatile and can be eaten raw, cooked in a pan or on the barbecue, dehydrated, deep-fried or baked. They make delicious soups, pâtés and risottos, can be added to casseroles and stuffed. Nick Femia, from South Australian Mushrooms, marinates his in dried oregano, garlic and extra-virgin olive oil for an hour before barbecuing. Or he marinates them in red wine vinegar, extra-virgin olive oil, garlic and thyme. Try mushrooms as a carpaccio with thinly sliced fennel and a little extra-virgin olive oil and lemon dressing. Or pop sliced Swiss browns on a baking tray, scatter herbs and your favourite cheese on top and pop under the grill (broiler). Sliced and cooked in butter with garlic then swirled with cream, mushrooms make the perfect pasta sauce. Use shimeji mushrooms in a stir-fry, soup or noodle dish. Oyster mushrooms are best quickly fried and complement most proteins while enoki can be eaten raw, look great in rice paper rolls and make a nice addition to omelettes or as a garnish on risotto, mushroom ragu or tempura.

Flat mushrooms

Enoki mushrooms

Oyster mushrooms

King brown mushrooms

Portobello mushrooms

Swiss brown mushrooms

Button mushrooms

Shimeji mushrooms

When I visited Paddy's Market in Sydney I met up with my old friend Jennice Kersh from Edna's Table. She had gathered a basket of goodies from the market and set me the challenge to create something. This is what I came up with!

MUSHROOM EGG NET

SERVES 4 as an appetiser

PREPARATION
10 minutes

COOKING
10 minutes

WINE

Mushrooms always have an affinity with pinot noir as they are both a bit earthy. Pinot noir can also handle chilli.

LYNDEY'S NOTE

Egg nets can also be sliced into bite-sized pieces and served as a canapé.

2 large red chillies
peanut or extra-virgin olive oil
1 teaspoon sesame oil
4 garlic cloves, finely chopped
130 g (4½ oz) white button mushrooms, sliced
130 g (4½ oz) Swiss brown mushrooms, sliced
1 bunch coriander (cilantro), roots and stems finely chopped and leaves picked

90 g (3 oz/1 cup) bean sprouts
1 tablespoon fish sauce
50 g (1¾ oz) palm sugar (jaggery)
4 eggs
35 g (1¼ oz) roasted peanuts, roughly chopped
1 spring onion (scallion), cut into thin matchsticks (optional)

Thinly slice one red chilli and seed and cut the other into thin matchsticks, reserving for garnish. Heat the peanut or olive oil and sesame oil in a large frying pan over medium heat. Add the garlic, chilli, mushrooms, coriander roots and stems and cook, stirring occasionally, for 2 minutes or until the mushrooms are soft and beginning to turn golden. Add the bean sprouts and sauté for 1 minute longer. Season with the fish sauce and palm sugar. Transfer the mixture to a bowl.

Whisk the eggs gently in a medium bowl. Do not overbeat. Pour the egg mixture into a pitcher or use a funnel to pour into a squeeze bottle.

Heat a little more oil in a large frying pan and wipe out leaving a thin coat. Place over medium heat and pour in one quarter of the egg mixture in thin streams from the pitcher or squeeze bottle, making a lattice pattern. Alternatively, dip your hand in the egg mix and move it backwards and forwards across the flat frying pan, dripping the egg so that it drizzles lines in the oil. Do not move too quickly otherwise the strands will be too fine and will break. Circle the perimeter to form a border on the net. Gently cook for 30–40 seconds or until the egg net is cooked through. Turn out onto a sheet of baking paper or a plate. Repeat until the egg mix is finished.

Divide the mushroom mixture down the centre of the nets and sprinkle with the peanuts and coriander leaves. Gently roll to encase. Alternatively, lay out an egg net, spread some mix on the lower third of the net and roll up. Repeat with the remaining nets and mixture. Garnish the egg nets with the spring onion, if using, and reserved chilli and serve immediately.

A perfect do-ahead canapé with two types of cooked mushrooms – oven-roasted and pan-fried – sitting on buttery brioche.

MUSHROOM CUSTARDS WITH BRIOCHE CRUMBS

MAKES 30 squares

PREPARATION 15 minutes

COOKING 1 hour 25 minutes

WINE

This dish is quite buttery and creamy so try a chardonnay or a pinot noir.

LYNDEY'S NOTE

These can be made ahead and reheated in a 140°C (275°F) oven. They can also be served cold or at room temperature.

5 eschalots, peeled
2 garlic cloves, peeled
500 g (1 lb 2 oz) mushrooms, a mixture of Swiss brown and button
2 teaspoons thyme leaves, plus extra to serve
2 tablespoons extra-virgin olive oil

1 loaf brioche, cut into 1 cm (½ in) slices
100 g (3½ oz) butter
salt and freshly ground black pepper to taste
250 g (9 oz/1 cup) sour cream
4 egg yolks

Preheat the oven to 180°C (350°F).

Using a food processor, finely chop the eschalots and garlic. Add half the mushrooms and the thyme and pulse until finely chopped. Spread the mushroom mixture onto a baking tray that has been lined with baking paper, drizzle with oil and bake for 1 hour, stirring occasionally.

Meanwhile, place the brioche slices on another lined baking tray and bake for 10 minutes or until dry and crisp. They may need to be turned halfway through cooking time. Process into crumbs using the food processor and add half the butter gradually until the texture resembles wet sand. Season to taste with salt and pepper. Press into the base of a lined baking tray (approximately 30 cm x 20 cm/12 in x 8 in) and bake for 10 minutes or until lightly golden.

Pulse the remaining mushrooms in the food processor until roughly chopped. Melt the remaining butter in a large frying pan, add the mushrooms and cook for 5 minutes or until golden. Set aside to cool.

Combine the cooled, baked mushrooms and fried mushrooms with the sour cream and egg yolks and mix until just combined. Season to taste with salt and pepper, pour over the brioche base and return to the oven and cook for a further 15 minutes until just set. Serve cut into fingers sprinkled with the extra thyme leaves.

Lyndey with Nick Femia of South Australian Mushrooms, in one of their impressive, specially designed, climate-controlled growing rooms.

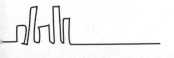

THE VINES

TOP LEFT: Lyndey Milan, Maggie Beer and Saskia Beer at Maggie's Farm in the Barossa Valley, South Australia.

TOP RIGHT: Grapes ripening on the vine.

BOTTOM: Lyndey on board a trike with Tony Tscharke from Barossa Unique Tours.

Australia is one of the great New World wine success stories. Around 149,000 hectares (368,000 acres) of grape vines with 2400 wineries in 65 wine regions produce 1.1 billion litres (240 million gallons) annually. Of this, 681 million litres (150 million gallons) are exported and 453 million (100 million gallons) are sold domestically, with over 30 million glasses of Australian wine consumed worldwide every day.

One of the regions most steeped in heritage and tradition is the Barossa Valley in South Australia and a trike tour is a great way to see it. Its Mediterranean climate provides the perfect conditions for growing not only grapes but all manner of produce. Food hero and long-time friend, Maggie Beer, has set the country on fire with her warm personality and passion for all things Barossa. I caught up with her and her artisanal food producer daughter, Saskia, over a glass of sparkling ruby cabernet (sparkling verjuice). They both feel strongly about the Barossa and the people who live and produce there and relish the great German traditions of the area, including curing and smoking meats, preserving fruits and making pickles.

The region has been producing wines for over 170 years with some of the soils reputed to be 300 million years old. Even the vines are some of the oldest in the world because they were never destroyed by phylloxera, which killed vines in France and other regions in Europe, North America and New Zealand.

World-famous wine label Jacob's Creek, widely recognised as spearheading this country's export growth, is also from the Barossa Valley. First released in 1976, Jacob's Creek has been the most popular brand in Australia and also our leading export brand for more than a decade. The Jacob's Creek Visitor Centre offers not only a restaurant and wine tasting, but master classes on matching wine with cheese or chocolate. There's even a display vineyard where, in season, you can taste and actually get the flavour of the wine in the grapes.

Closer to Adelaide, the cool climate of the Adelaide Hills is well suited to wine styles like sauvignon blanc, pinot noir and also tempranillo. Mount Lofty House was built in the Victorian era between 1852 and 1858 but was almost completely destroyed by the Ash Wednesday bushfires in the early 1980s – bushfires being a constant threat in many parts of Australia. Fortunately it has been rebuilt to retain the original charm, beautifully offset by 4.8 hectares (12 acres) of gardens and vineyards – and it's a great location to stay and cook.

In the smallest mainland state of Australia, Victoria, the Yarra Valley is only just over an hour's drive from Melbourne. Also with a cool climate ideal for growing premium wines, it's a stunning region for pinot noir, and is seen by aficionados like my friends Steve Webber and Leanne De Bortoli as the Holy Grail for winemakers.

Yet there's much more than grapevines in the Yarra. On the outskirts is a salmon farm with over 50,000 fish in 16 ponds. The Rubicon River is fed by both springs and melting snow so the water runs at 6°C (43°F), which salmon love. It's one of the only freshwater aquaculture farms in the world, and the only one in Australia, to use a natural method of harvesting the roe. Every May 20,000 salmon are hand-milked. I've tried it a couple of times with Nick Gorman from Yarra Valley Caviar and was determined to go back for the TV show. The mature fish are anaesthetised with clove oil in baths, then the roe is gently massaged by hand from their stomachs before the fish are revived in a highly oxygenated bath. The salmon eggs are then cleaned, hand-picked, immersed in a salt–sugar solution and pasteurised.

Yering, in the heart of the Yarra Valley is a place of lush pastures, where the quality of the milk allows cheesemakers like Jack Holman at Yarra Valley Dairy to produce the finest cheese. A dairy for 100 years, it has been a cheesery with café attached for around 20, with Persian Fetta their flagship product.

The TarraWarra Museum of Art in Healesville, opened a decade ago, is one of the world's leading exhibitors of significant Australian and international works of art. Art curator Victoria Lynn (whose father lectured me in fine arts at university) showed me around the stunning building.

In the Hunter Valley in New South Wales, from humble beginnings four generations of McGuigan winemakers have helped to put Australian wine on the world map. And these days, raconteur and all-round good guy, Neil McGuigan, is at the helm – three-time winner of international winemaker of the year. Here it is the high humidity and proximity to the coast which makes the Hunter unique, especially for semillon, shiraz and chardonnay.

Orange in the Central Tablelands of New South Wales has always been at the forefront of regional food, and celebrates with an annual festival. There is a F.O.O.D (Food of Orange District) train that leaves from Central Station in Sydney for the annual F.O.O.D Week in April. This is a fun way to get there while sampling the produce from producers on board, who explain it is the cool climate from high altitude that makes it easy to grow great produce. And not only plants. At egganic, an organic egg farm, 2500 Isa Brown chickens roam free, guarded by the Italian breed of Maremma sheepdogs, which keep predators at bay so the hens can lay 160 dozen eggs daily. Bees flourish too with 40,000–50,000 per hive at the Beekeeper's Inn, once a Cobb and Co Inn in the 1880s, which has a café, tasting room, museum and even a brewery.

Borrodell on the Mount, one of the highest vineyards in Australia, holds a Black Tie Truffle Hunt and Gumboot Dinner every winter. We foraged for truffles from inoculated trees first planted some 20 years ago. The truffle industry in Australia is growing rapidly right across the country. So, too, is the olive oil industry, and olive groves often follow where vines have gone before. Yet each region is intrinsically different, moulded not only by the climate and growing conditions, but by what people do, too – and the odd accident. The Hansen family got a few deer to control blackberries on their farm just out of Orange 35 years ago, and now the blackberries are still thriving but there are some 2000 head of deer, with son Tim starting the Mandagery Creek Venison brand about 12 years ago, a free-range, premium product for the table.

The first payable gold was found nearby in the Ophir goldfields. The goldrush town of Millthorpe, established in the early 1900s and classified by the National Trust, is a piece of living history. Full of cobbled streets with bluestone borders and old buildings, it also houses a top restaurant called Tonic.

Just southwest of Orange, Canowindra is the hot air balloon capital of Australia and holds one of the biggest balloon events in the country. The annual Balloon Glow and Night Markets are quite a spectacle and a great way to trial more local produce – but in the early morning the bird's eye view of the region from a balloon is unforgettable.

Across the other side of the country, the Margaret River Wine region is about a three and a half hour drive south from Perth. Once a chilled-out surfie town renowned for some of the best big-wave surfing in the world, it has grown a new reputation for premium wines, since such pioneers as Kevin and Diana Cullen first planted grapes in 1966. Their daughter Vanya, a dear friend, is now in the hot seat and has moved the property to becoming biodynamic, winning innumerable accolades. Even when I have visited previously in the middle of winter, her vines have a life and vibrancy to them. This time I delighted in her biodynamic garden, using its bounty to cook with.

The area is also host to the Margaret River Gourmet Escape, an annual festival featuring over 25 international and Australian food and wine celebrities. Here I rubbed shoulders with the likes of Heston Blumenthal, chatted with Guillaume Brahimi on Smiths Beach as he cooked a barbecue lunch, met up with Julien Royer – chef at JAAN in Singapore – before he went on stage, learned about foraging from local Wardandi educator Josh Whiteland and roamed the gourmet village tasting truffles and other local delicacies, interviewing producers and catching up with old friends. Two of these, Tetsuya Wakuda from Tetsuya's in Sydney and Waku Ghin in Singapore, and Shane Osborn, Perth-born head chef at St Betty in Hong Kong, collaborated with winery Voyager Estate's executive chef, Nigel Harvey, on an inspiring dinner menu using unique Western Australian produce with matching wines. This was rounded off by a chat from one of the world's most influential restaurant reviewers AA Gill. What a festival!

But there's plenty to see at other times of the year and the monthly farmers' market is not to be missed. In addition to the usual fresh produce, organic eggs, fruit and vegetables there was the most outstanding display of WA wildflowers, as well as a most engaging Italian pastry chef. Here too I met up with David Hohnen, whom I knew years ago at Cape Mentelle winery, now a free-range sheep and pig farmer at The Farm House with his Big Red pigs. I was also pleased to make new friends, like Josh Bahen, a winemaker for 10 years, but now a chocolatier par excellence, honourably sourcing cocoa beans direct from farmers in poor communities, teaching them along the way and then working them in small batches in rare vintage machines.

I opened this episode at Prevelly Beach where the Margaret River meets the Indian Ocean, introducing Tetsuya and Josh Bahen and finished it canoeing with Sean Blocksidge from the Margaret River Discovery Company into the sunset along the river itself.

I created this on Sydney's Central Station, as a welcome breakfast to the folk on the F.O.O.D train to Orange, which I hosted. I used local produce from Orange and it was washed down with local wine. Quark, a fresh, set cheese with a slight acidic taste, is made by straining warm soured milk.

MELON WITH SPARKLING SPICED DRIZZLE, QUARK AND PISTACHIO NUTS

SERVES 4 as part of a breakfast or brunch buffet

PREPARATION
15 minutes

WINE
Sparkling wine from the high-quality, cool climate of Orange is ideal for a celebratory breakfast.

LYNDEY'S NOTE
If melons are out of season, other fruit, such as berries, pears, pineapple or stone fruit, can be substituted. You can substitute thick yoghurt for the quark.

200 g (7 oz) seedless watermelon, rind removed
200 g (7 oz) rockmelon (cantaloupe/netted melon), rind and seeds removed
2 small figs, halved
120 g (4½ oz) quark
mint or basil leaves, torn, to serve
35 g (1¼ oz/¼ cup) roughly chopped pistachio nuts, lightly toasted, to serve

SPARKLING SPICED DRIZZLE
125 ml (4 fl oz/½ cup) water
115 g (4 oz/½ cup) caster (superfine) sugar
⅓ large red chilli, seeded and sliced
½ teaspoon ground ginger
½ teaspoon freshly ground black pepper
1 teaspoon vanilla bean paste
60 ml (2 fl oz/¼ cup) sparkling wine

For the sparkling spiced drizzle, combine the water and caster sugar in a small saucepan. Cook over medium heat until the sugar dissolves. Bring to the boil and simmer for 5 minutes. Set aside to cool before using.

While the syrup is cooling, pound the chilli, ginger, black pepper and vanilla bean paste using a mortar and pestle until smooth. Add 1 tablespoon of the sugar syrup and the sparkling wine and mix until combined. (The left-over sugar syrup can be used in cocktails or dressings.)

Cut each wedge of watermelon and rockmelon into slices. Place a few slices each of watermelon and rockmelon and a fig half into individual serving dishes, drizzle with the sparkling spiced drizzle and top with a spoonful of quark, the torn mint leaves and the pistachio nuts.

This recipe celebrates the beautiful salmon pearls from Yarra Valley Caviar salmon. It can be made with fresh, poached or even smoked salmon.

PRAWN CRACKERS WITH SALMON, SALMON ROE AND NORI

MAKES 12

PREPARATION 10 minutes

COOKING 5 minutes

WINE

This is best matched with a sparkling wine, as the bubbles in the wine reflect the 'bubbles' of the salmon roe.

LYNDEY'S NOTE

Prawn crackers and toasted nori (in both sheet and finely chopped form) are available in the Asian aisle of your supermarket, or in Japanese food stores.

oil for deep-frying
12 prawn crackers
60 g (2 oz/¼ cup) yoghurt, crème fraîche or light sour cream
1 teaspoon wasabi
250 g (9 oz) skinless, pinboned salmon fillet, raw or poached, diced or flaked

1 small (50 g/1¾ oz) jar of salmon roe
1 small nashi pear (or crisp apple), finely diced
dill sprigs or baby mustard cress
toasted nori pieces

Heat the oil in a deep-fryer until hot. Drop in the prawn crackers. They should puff up, expand and rise to the top immediately. Drain well on paper towel.

Combine the yoghurt and wasabi and gently mix through the salmon. Lay the prawn crackers on a serving platter. In the middle of each cracker place about a tablespoon of salmon mixture, a teaspoon of salmon roe, a teaspoon of nashi, some dill or snipped mustard cress and some nori pieces.

Snails Bon Appetite are farmed in the Congewai Valley in the Hunter Valley, New South Wales, with a growers' network in other parts of Australia. Common garden snails, they are farmed and purged before harvest and are available in the shell, or boiled, shelled and vacuum-packed.

SNAILS IN HERBED CREAM SAUCE ON GARLIC CRUMBS

MAKES 12

PREPARATION
10 minutes

COOKING
25 minutes

WINE
These buttery, creamy bites are well matched with a Hunter Valley chardonnay.

salt
white wine vinegar
12 snails in the shell
20 g (¾ oz) butter
1 eschalot, finely chopped
60 ml (2 fl oz/¼ cup) dry white wine
60 ml (2 fl oz/¼ cup) thickened
   (whipping) cream

1 tablespoon finely chopped
   tarragon leaves
salt and freshly ground black pepper

GARLIC CRUMBS
20 g (¾ oz) butter
1 garlic clove, finely chopped
40 g (1½ oz/½ cup) brioche crumbs
1½ tablespoons finely chopped chives

Bring a large saucepan of water to the boil with some salt and a splash of white wine vinegar. Add the whole snails and cook for 15 minutes. Refresh in iced water to stop the cooking process, then shell the snails.

Melt the butter in a medium frying pan over medium–low heat. Add the eschalot and cook until softened but not browned, for a couple of minutes. Add the wine and cream and simmer for 5 minutes or until thickened.

Add the tarragon and snails, season with salt and pepper and cook over medium heat for a minute or two more.

Meanwhile, for the garlic crumbs, melt the butter in a small frying pan over medium heat, whisking frequently. When the butter foams, add the garlic and brioche crumbs and stir until brown and aromatic. Remove from the heat and add the chives.

To serve, place some garlic crumbs in the bottom of individual canapé spoons then spoon the snails and their sauce on top and serve immediately.

Brook trout is a large freshwater fish related to salmon and trout. If you can't get it, use rainbow trout, though this is much thinner and will cook more quickly. I cooked this dish in the most sublime location, beside the bubbling river at Yarra Valley Caviar farm.

STEAMED BROOK TROUT WITH SALMON CAVIAR

SERVES 4

PREPARATION
10 minutes

COOKING 10 minutes

WINE

The lovely citrus flavours cry out for a semillon or riesling, which can both handle the chilli as they are unwooded.

180 g (6½ oz) bean-thread (cellophane) noodles
3 lemongrass stems, halved lengthways
4 spring onions (scallions), halved
6 fresh kaffir lime leaves, crushed
4 cm (1½ in) piece fresh ginger, sliced
3 garlic cloves, halved
500 ml (17 fl oz/2 cups) fish stock, or more, depending on size of pan

4 x 180 g (6½ oz) fillets brook or rainbow trout
2 red bird's eye chillies, thinly sliced
280 g (10 oz) snow peas (mangetout)
3 fresh limes
½ teaspoon Thai fish sauce, or more to taste
2 tablespoons salmon caviar
½ cup coriander (cilantro) leaves

Place the bean-thread noodles in a bowl and cover with boiling water to soften for about 5 minutes.

Choose a large, deep-sided frying pan with a lid, that will just fit the aromatics so they can form a 'raft' on which to place the fish, so it can steam. To the pan, add the lemongrass and spring onions and scatter around the kaffir lime leaves, ginger and garlic, then gently pour over the fish stock. Bring to the boil over high heat. Place the fish fillets on top, scatter with the chilli, reduce the heat to a simmer and cover with the lid. Cook for 5 minutes or until the fish is opaque at the edges and still pink in the middle. Scatter the snow peas around the pan in the last minute of cooking, if there is room, otherwise steam or blanch them separately for a minute or two.

To serve, drain the noodles and divide between four bowls. Place the fish fillets on top. Stir the juice of 1 lime and the fish sauce through the fish stock and then discard the lemongrass, kaffir lime leaves, ginger and garlic. Taste and add more lime juice and fish sauce if necessary. Ladle the stock and snow peas around the fish. Top the fish with a heaped teaspoon of the salmon caviar and scatter over the coriander. Serve immediately with an extra lime cheek.

Amanda Walker, one of the hosts on the F.O.O.D (Food of Orange District) train, made these with a clever technique for baking them rather than deep-frying. I prefer using prosciutto to bacon but, either way, these eggs are perfect for a picnic breakfast or anytime.

PROSCIUTTO-WRAPPED SCOTCH EGGS

MAKES 12

PREPARATION
15 minutes

COOKING
30 minutes

WINE

These Scotch eggs are perfect picnic food and softer styles of red wine are great picnic wines, so try a barbera, sangiovese or pinot noir.

13 free-range eggs
5 slices white bread, crusts removed
200 ml (7 fl oz) milk
500 g (1 lb 2 oz) minced (ground) pork
500 g (1 lb 2 oz) minced (ground) veal
2 tablespoons finely chopped flat-leaf (Italian) parsley

1 tablespoon thyme leaves
½ teaspoon freshly grated nutmeg
salt and freshly ground black pepper
12 prosciutto slices or very thin bacon rashers (slices)
rocket (arugula) to serve
tomato chutney to serve

Preheat the oven to 170°C (340°F). Lightly oil 12 holes (170 ml/5½ fl oz/⅔ cup capacity) in a large-sized muffin tin.

Place 12 of the eggs into a saucepan of hot water and bring to the boil. Stir to ensure the egg yolks will centre in the white. Simmer for 5 minutes from the time the water starts to bubble. Drain the eggs and run under cold water until cool. Peel carefully.

Soak the bread in the milk for 1 minute. Drain and squeeze dry. Place the bread and minces into a large bowl and use your hands to combine. Then add the remaining egg, the parsley, thyme and nutmeg and season with salt and pepper. Mix to combine evenly and divide into 12 balls.

Press the mince mixture firmly around each egg, ensuring the entire egg is covered. Then wrap a piece of prosciutto around the middle of each egg and place them into the prepared muffin tin.

Bake for 25 minutes until nicely browned. Allow to cool for a few minutes before draining on paper towel. Serve halved, warm or cold, with rocket and tomato chutney.

Nepenthe Wines in the Adelaide Hills has been experimenting with Spanish wine varieties, so I was inspired to create some tapas, which I matched with winemaker Alex Trescowthick's latest vintages. I also served some local goat's cheese, toasted thinly sliced baguette and blanched asparagus to go with his sauvignon blanc.

ADELAIDE HILLS SPANISH TAPAS

SPICED PORK ROLLS

MAKES 16

PREPARATION
10 minutes

COOKING 5 minutes

WINE

Try the softer, more fruit-driven characters of tempranillo, which can handle the spice!

250 g (9 oz) minced (ground) pork
½ small red onion, finely chopped
1 garlic clove, finely chopped
1 teaspoon smoked Spanish paprika
2 teaspoons dry sherry

15 g (½ oz/¼ cup) stale breadcrumbs
salt and freshly ground black pepper
60 g (2 oz) prosciutto (about 4 slices)
extra-virgin olive oil for shallow-frying
toothpicks to secure rolls

Combine all the ingredients, except the prosciutto and oil, in a large bowl. Mix until very well combined. Roll a tablespoon of the mixture into a sausage shape then repeat with the remaining mixture.

Cut each slice of prosciutto into four lengthways, and then across to create rectangle shapes. Roll each pork sausage in a piece of prosciutto and secure with a toothpick.

Heat the oil in a large frying pan to a depth of 2 cm (¾ in) and fry the sausages, turning from time to time, for 5 minutes or until golden brown and cooked through. Drain on paper towel.

PINOT NOIR MUSHROOMS

MAKES 12

PREPARATION
10 minutes

COOKING
20 minutes

WINE

If food is cooked in a wine, it makes the perfect match to drink with it!

20 g (¾ oz) butter
2 garlic cloves, finely chopped
120 g (4½ oz) button mushrooms
   (about 12)

125 ml (4 fl oz/½ cup) pinot noir
125 ml (4 fl oz/½ cup) chicken stock
3 thyme sprigs, plus extra to serve

Melt the butter in a medium frying pan over high heat. Add the garlic and mushrooms and sauté for 3 minutes. Add the pinot noir, stock and thyme and simmer gently for 15 minutes, or until the liquid is absorbed and the mushrooms are tender. Serve at room temperature, topped with the extra thyme sprigs.

This was my contribution to a five-course truffle degustation dinner at the annual Black Tie Truffle Hunt and Gumboot Dinner at Borodell on the Mount in Orange. It works just as well at home — with or without the truffle!

TWICE-BAKED CHEESE AND TRUFFLE SOUFFLÉ

SERVES 10 as part of a degustation or 5 as an appetiser

PREPARATION
15 minutes, plus a few days to infuse the eggs with truffle

COOKING
40 minutes, plus cooling

WINE

The beautiful savoury umami flavours of these soufflés are best matched with a chardonnay or viognier.

4 eggs
10 g (¼ oz) truffle, plus extra truffle for shaving
25 g (1 oz) butter, melted, plus 50 g (1¾ oz) butter extra
320 ml (11 fl oz) milk
pinch of freshly grated nutmeg
1 bay leaf

6 black peppercorns
35 g (1¼ oz/¼ cup) plain (all-purpose) flour
120 g (4½ oz) grated gruyère, plus 40 g (1½ oz) diced gruyére
salt and freshly ground black pepper
125 ml (4 fl oz/½ cup) pouring (single/ light) cream (36% fat)

Several days prior to cooking, place the eggs in an airtight jar with the truffle to infuse the flavour.

Clean the truffle, then peel it carefully and reserve the peel. Finely chop the truffle. Separate the eggs and place the chopped truffle in a bowl with the egg yolks.

Preheat the oven to 200°C (400°F). Brush the insides of ten 60 ml (2 fl oz/¼ cup) ramekins with the melted butter.

Heat the milk in a small saucepan with the truffle peelings, nutmeg, bay leaf and peppercorns and bring slowly to a simmer over low heat. Remove from the heat, cover and stand to infuse for 15 minutes, until cooled. Drain, discarding the solids.

Make a roux by melting the extra 50 g (1¾ oz) butter in a small saucepan over low heat and stirring in the flour. Cook, stirring constantly, for 1–2 minutes, until it smells nutty and is lightly golden brown. Remove from the heat and gradually add the strained milk, whisking as you go. Return to medium heat, stirring constantly until very thick and boiling. Reduce the heat to low and stir for another 5 minutes, to thicken further. Beat in 40 g (1½ oz) of the grated cheese and the truffle and egg yolk mixture. Season to taste.

»»»

LYNDEY'S NOTE

If cooking in larger ramekins for an appetiser, increase the first cooking time by about 5 minutes.

Whisk the egg whites in a clean bowl using an electric mixer until foamy, add a pinch of salt and beat until just stiff. Fold gently into the cheese and egg yolk mixture with the diced cheese in two batches. Fill the prepared ramekins to the top, levelling them by scraping with the back of a knife across the top. Clean the rims and place the ramekins in a large baking dish. Place on an oven shelf and add enough boiling water to the baking dish to come halfway up the sides of the ramekins. Bake for 10–15 minutes, until well risen. The tops should feel soft and springy to the touch.

Remove from the baking dish and allow to cool completely. They will sink a little. The soufflés can be prepared to this stage, wrapped in plastic wrap and kept refrigerated or frozen if desired.

Preheat the oven to 200°C (400°F).

Turn the soufflés out of the dishes onto a baking tray lined with baking paper – the topside can be up or turned over to make the base. Drizzle the soufflés with the cream and the remaining grated cheese. Bake for 10 minutes (or a few minutes longer if they have been frozen) or until well risen. Shave an extra slice or two of truffle on top and serve immediately.

This was made from local rabbit by chef Tony Worland from Tonic Restaurant in Millthorpe, New South Wales. It is a play on a French boudin blanc, which is usually made with chicken or pork.

RABBIT BOUDIN WITH BROAD BEANS, PEAS AND VICHYSSOISE SAUCE

SERVES 6–8

PREPARATION
20 minutes

COOKING
20 minutes

WINE
Try a white wine with texture, like chardonnay or pinot gris, or a rosé.

LYNDEY'S NOTE
This mixture can make little or large burger patties, too.

RABBIT BOUDIN
500 g (1 lb 2 oz) minced (ground) rabbit
4 egg yolks
1 tablespoon fresh tarragon, finely chopped
salt and freshly ground black pepper
400 ml (13½ fl oz) pouring (single/light) cream
fresh sausage skins
1 tablespoon extra-virgin olive oil

VICHYSSOISE SAUCE
1 tablespoon extra-virgin olive oil
20 g (¾ oz) butter
2 leeks, chopped
2 garlic cloves, finely chopped
3 all-purpose potatoes, such as desiree, peeled and diced

250 ml (8½ fl oz/1 cup) chicken stock
sea salt
100 ml (3½ fl oz) pouring (single/light) cream
2 teaspoons truffle oil
freshly ground black pepper

GREENS
20 g (¾ oz) butter
95 g (3¼ oz/½ cup) broad (fava) beans, blanched
100 g (3½ oz/⅔ cup) fresh peas
2 tarragon sprigs
1 bunch pea tendrils, washed

crisp pancetta to serve
freshly shaved black truffle to serve (optional)

Put the rabbit in a bowl over a larger bowl of ice and add the egg yolks one by one. Add the tarragon, season to taste, then gently fold in the cream. Place the mixture in a piping bag and pipe into the sausage skins. Tie the sausages with string to the desired lengths and place in a steamer. Steam slowly until the sausages become firm, around 15 minutes. Remove from the steamer and set aside to cool, then place in the refrigerator to set.

For the sauce, melt the oil and butter in a pan over medium heat. Add the leek and garlic and sweat until soft. Add the potatoes, cover with the stock and add some sea salt. When the potatoes are cooked, blend and finish with the cream, truffle oil and salt and pepper.

In a heavy-based frying pan, heat the olive oil and fry the boudin slowly for a few minutes, turning until warm and lightly golden. If the pan is too hot, the boudin will split. For the greens, in a separate frying pan, heat the butter then add the greens to warm. To serve, spread the vichyssoise on the base of a serving plate, top with the greens, boudin and the pancetta and truffle, if using.

I cooked this recipe with Sophie Hansen from Mandagery Creek Venison in Orange. It is adapted from one by Martin Boetz, long-time chef at Longrain and now with his own venture, the Cooks Co-op. It was at Longrain, over this dish, that Sophie met her husband, Tim. I was there, too and, as Sophie and I had become close when she worked for me, it was very special to be there.

VENISON MASSAMAN CURRY

SERVES 4

PREPARATION
15 minutes

COOKING 2 hours
10 minutes

WINE

A curry like this with coconut milk works fantastically with a shiraz that has been in American oak, as this can give the same coconut character. Try one from the Barossa Valley.

LYNDEY'S NOTE

Store any excess paste in a clean, airtight jar in the refrigerator for up to 6 months. Roasting the shrimp paste really brings out the flavour. Simply wrap it in foil and roast in the oven for 5 minutes or toast it in a frying pan.

1 x 400 ml (13½ fl oz) tin coconut cream
2 tablespoons extra-virgin olive oil (optional)
400–450 g (14 oz–1 lb) venison osso buco
1 teaspoon palm sugar (jaggery)
40–60 ml (1¼–2 fl oz) fish sauce to taste
60–100 g (2–3½ oz) tamarind purée to taste
5 bay leaves
5 cardamon pods, toasted
1 large sweet potato, peeled and cut into 2 cm (¾ in) dice
steamed rice to serve
80 g (2¾ oz/½ cup) unsalted roasted peanuts, chopped, to serve
½ cup fresh coriander (cilantro) leaves, coarsely chopped, to serve

MASSAMAN CURRY PASTE
2 teaspoons ground coriander
¼ teaspoon ground cloves
1 teaspoon ground cinnamon
2 teaspoons ground cumin
1 teaspoon shrimp paste, roasted
3 garlic cloves, finely chopped
1 brown onion (about 150 g/5½ oz), chopped
8 large red chillies, seeded and roughly chopped
1 lemongrass stem, trimmed, white part chopped
3 cm (1¼ in) piece fresh galangal, peeled and chopped

To make the curry paste, blend the coriander, cloves, cinnamon, cumin, shrimp paste and 1 tablespoon or more of cold water until smooth. Add the remaining ingredients, one at a time, blending well after each addition until the mixture forms a thick paste. This makes 125 g (4½ oz/½ cup).

To make the curry, preheat the oven to 160°C (320°F). Place a wok or heavy saucepan over medium–high heat. If the coconut cream has risen to the top of the tin, just add this, otherwise pour in 60 ml (2 fl oz/¼ cup) coconut milk and cook, stirring constantly for 3–5 minutes, until it separates. If it does not separate, add the optional oil. Add 60 g (2 oz/¼ cup) of the curry paste and fry, stirring constantly until fragrant, for 1–2 minutes.

Add the venison to the paste and brown for 2–3 minutes. Add the remaining coconut milk, reserving 2 tablespoons for garnish later. Increase the heat and bring to the boil. Add the palm sugar, fish sauce, tamarind purée, bay leaves and cardamom pods and return to the boil. If necessary, add 100 ml (3½ fl oz) or so of water to almost cover the venison and keep it moist. Cover and cook in the oven for 1 hour or until the venison is nearly tender. Add the sweet potato, cover and return to the oven for a further hour or until the potato is tender. Serve with steamed rice topped with the chopped roasted peanuts, remaining thick coconut cream and the coriander.

I cooked this in a Hunter Valley vineyard with Neil McGuigan of the famed McGuigan wine dynasty, specifically to go with his 2005 Bin 9000 Semillon.

LEMON POACHED CHICKEN WITH SILVERBEET RISOTTO AND HERBED TOMATO DRESSING

SERVES 4

PREPARATION
15 minutes

COOKING
25 minutes

1.25 litres (42 fl oz/5 cups) chicken stock
60 ml (2 fl oz/¼ cup) extra-virgin olive oil
40 g (1½ oz) butter
1 leek, washed and thinly sliced
2 garlic cloves, finely chopped
440 g (15½ oz/2 cups) arborio or other risotto rice
125 ml (4 fl oz/½ cup) white wine
4 stalks silverbeet (Swiss chard), leaves only, washed and shredded
salt and freshly ground black pepper

LEMON POACHED CHICKEN
500 ml (17 fl oz/2 cups) chicken consommé
zest of 1 lemon, peeled with a vegetable peeler
4 garlic cloves, bruised

8 thyme sprigs
salt and freshly ground black pepper
3–4 boneless, skinless chicken breasts (about 800 g/1 lb 12 oz)

HERBED TOMATO DRESSING
⅓ cup chopped mixed herbs, such as thyme, flat-leaf (Italian) parsley, chives or mint
finely grated zest of 1 lemon
90 g (3 oz/½ cup) green olives, pitted and sliced
80 ml (2½ fl oz/⅓ cup) extra-virgin olive oil
1–2 tablespoons verjuice or lemon juice
100 g (3½ oz) baby roma (plum) tomatoes (assorted colours if available), halved or quartered if large

To make the risotto, heat the stock in a saucepan over medium heat until it is just simmering. Reduce the heat and maintain at a simmer. Alternatively, heat the stock in a pitcher in the microwave. Heat the oil and half the butter in a large heavy-based frying pan over medium heat. When the butter has melted, add the leek and fry for a minute or two without browning. Add the garlic and cook, stirring frequently, for a minute more. Add the rice and stir well to coat with the oil and butter (it will take on a glassy appearance). Add the wine and stir until it has evaporated.

»»»

This recipe was especially designed to go with Hunter Valley semillon – hence the lemon flavours and tomato in the dressing. Why not keep Neil happy and drink his wine!

Reduce the heat to low and add one ladleful of hot stock. Stir constantly until the liquid has been completely absorbed. Keep adding the stock, a ladleful at a time, stirring and waiting until it has been completely absorbed by the rice before adding the next ladle. Keep it cooking at a low simmer. After about 15 minutes taste a few grains of rice and stir through the silverbeet. When cooked, the rice should be tender, not soft, yet still a little firm to the bite. It will probably take around 20–25 minutes to reach this point. When the risotto is ready it should still be a little liquid, not dry like fried rice. Season to taste with salt and pepper and stir through the remaining butter.

Meanwhile, poach the chicken by combining the consommé, lemon zest, garlic, thyme and salt and pepper in a large saucepan over high heat. Add the chicken and top up with water to cover. Stir. Bring to the boil then reduce the heat to medium and poach the chicken for 15 minutes or until cooked through. Turn off the heat and allow to rest in the liquid for a further 5 minutes. (Reserve the delicious poaching liquid as flavoursome chicken stock to use in another recipe.)

For the herbed tomato dressing, pound the herbs well using a mortar and pestle. Add the lemon zest and olives and pound until combined. Mix through the oil and verjuice, then lightly crush the tomatoes and mix to combine.

To serve, ladle the risotto into serving bowls. Cut the chicken into strips or medallions, place them on top of the risotto and finally drizzle on the herbed tomato dressing.

The herb and vegie garden near the historic Jacob's Creek cottages in the Barossa Valley was not only a great setting to cook this recipe, but it also provided me with some greens from the garden to go with the other local produce.

BAROSSA VALLEY CHICKEN WITH VERJUICE

SERVES 4–6

PREPARATION
15 minutes

COOKING
55 minutes

WINE
This simply flavoured recipe matches surprisingly well with a white sparkling wine from Jacob's Creek.

1 whole 1.8–2 kg (4 lb–4 lb 6 oz) free-range Barossa Valley chicken
30 g (1 oz) butter, softened
1½ tablespoons chopped mixed herbs, such as flat-leaf (Italian) parsley, chives, sage and thyme
1 teaspoon dijon mustard
1 garlic clove, finely chopped, plus 2 garlic bulbs, top quarter sliced off
salt and freshly ground black pepper
1 tablespoon extra-virgin olive oil
80 ml (2½ fl oz/⅓ cup) verjuice
250 ml (8½ fl oz/1 cup) chicken stock
300 g (10½ oz/1⅔ cups) seedless green grapes
cress or micro herbs to serve

PARSNIP PURÉE
3 parsnips (about 750 g/1 lb 11 oz), peeled and chopped
100–200 ml (3½–7 fl oz) milk (depending on size of saucepan)
40 g (1½ oz) butter
salt and freshly ground black pepper

GARDEN SALAD
2 teaspoons walnut or extra-virgin olive oil
2 teaspoons verjuice
salt and freshly ground black pepper
100 g (3½ oz/2 cups) mixed salad leaves, including baby English spinach, pea shoots and mustard greens
40 g (1½ oz/⅓ cup) walnut pieces, toasted

Preheat the oven to 200°C (400°F).

Place the chicken, breast side down, on a chopping board and butterfly by cutting down one side of the backbone with kitchen scissors or a sharp knife. Cut down the other side and remove the backbone to a large baking tray. Turn over the chicken, breast side up, and press down firmly using your hands to flatten out. Gently push your fingers under the skin at the cavity end and continue to ease the skin away from the flesh using your fingers to the end of the breast and down to the thighs.

Combine the butter, herbs, mustard and chopped garlic. Carefully push this mixture under the chicken skin. Press on top of the skin to smooth the paste all over the breasts and down to the thighs. Season well all over with salt and pepper. Place the chicken, skin side up, on top of the backbone in the baking tray, tuck in the garlic bulbs, drizzle it all with oil and roast for 50 minutes or until the juices run clear when the thigh is pierced.

»»»

While the chicken is roasting, make the parsnip purée. Place the parsnips in a large saucepan with just enough milk to almost cover. Bring to the boil, reduce the heat to a simmer, cover and cook for approximately 15 minutes or until tender. Remove from the heat, add the butter and season with salt and pepper. Purée with a hand-held blender until smooth. Keep warm.

Remove the chicken and garlic to a serving platter and cover with foil to keep warm and rest. Remove the excess fat from the pan juices, place on the stovetop over high heat and, when bubbling, add the verjuice, chicken stock and grapes. Bring to the boil and simmer for 5 minutes or until well reduced. Discard the backbone. Season to taste with salt and pepper. Add any juices from the rested chicken.

Make the garden salad by whisking together the walnut oil, verjuice and salt and pepper in a bowl. Add the salad leaves and walnuts and toss through.

To serve, carve the chicken and serve with the parsnip purée, garden salad and sauce.

My friend Saskia Beer not only produces glorious Barossa Valley chicken in her Barossa Farm Produce range, but also pork from Heritage Black Berkshire pigs, grown with the same 'paddock to plate' philosophy of low-impact farming and stress-free pastures. This is my adaptation of one of her recipes.

PORK CUTLETS WITH LEMON, CAPERS AND PARSLEY

SERVES 4

PREPARATION
15 minutes

COOKING
25 minutes

WINE
Pork has a natural affinity with pinot gris, as the textures work well together.

LYNDEY'S NOTE
Vincotto, literally 'cooked wine', is made from grape must. It has an appealing sweet and sour flavour and can be used in sweet or savoury dishes.

4 pork cutlets, skin on (about 900 g/2 lb) bones French-trimmed (you can ask your butcher to do this for you)
salt and freshly ground black pepper
20 g (¾ oz) butter
1 tablespoon extra-virgin olive oil
2 garlic cloves, finely chopped
2 teaspoons finely grated lemon zest
2 tablespoons lemon juice
50 g (1¾ oz/¼ cup) capers (preferably in salt), rinsed and drained

170 ml (5½ fl oz/⅔ cup) chicken stock
¼ cup flat-leaf (Italian) parsley, roughly chopped

ROCKET AND BASIL SALAD
90 g (3 oz/2 cups) rocket (arugula)
250 g (9 oz) cherry tomatoes, halved
1 eschalot, thinly sliced
½ bunch basil, roughly torn
1 tablespoon vincotto
1 tablespoon lemon juice
1½ tablespoons extra-virgin olive oil

Preheat the oven to 200°C (400°F) and line a large baking tray with baking paper.

Trim the skin off the pork cutlets, leaving a thin layer of fat. Cut the skin into pieces, toss in salt and pepper to taste and roast in the oven on the baking tray until it becomes crackling. It will take around 20 minutes or so and should be done by the time you have cooked the rest of the recipe.

Season the pork with salt and pepper to taste. Preheat a frying pan over medium heat and add half the butter and all the oil. When the butter melts and foams, swirl around to cover the base of the pan then add the pork and cook for a minute or two on each side, depending on thickness, until golden. Reserve the pan for the sauce.

Reduce the oven temperature to 180°C (350°F) then place the cutlets on the tray with the crackling and return to the oven for 5 minutes or until just cooked. Remove the pork cutlets to a warm plate and cover loosely with foil to rest. Turn the oven temperature back up to 200°C (400°F) and return the crackling to the oven while the pork is resting, and cook until really crisp.

Add the garlic, lemon zest and juice, capers and chicken stock to the reserved pan, place over high heat and allow to bubble up. Stir through the parsley and any juices from the pork. Whisk through the remaining butter. Season to taste with salt and pepper.

For the salad, place the rocket, tomatoes, eschalot and basil in a large bowl. Combine the vincotto, lemon juice and oil to make a dressing and mix through the salad gently to combine before serving. Serve the pork cutlets with the sauce and salad.

PORK STEAKS WITH NETTLE SAUCE, PICKLE, ASPARAGUS AND BROAD BEAN SALAD

SERVES 4

PREPARATION
10 minutes

COOKING 10 minutes

WINE

Try a Margaret River chardonnay match for this Margaret River produce. Chardonnay has enough texture to marry with the pork, and can also handle the sweet/sour of the pickle.

LYNDEY'S NOTE

Stinging nettles lose their sting once they are cooked. But use gloves until you put them in the pan!

1 tablespoon extra-virgin olive oil
20 g (¾ oz) butter
8 pork leg steaks (about 800 g/1 lb 12 oz)
salt
125 ml (4 fl oz/½ cup) dry white wine
12 stinging nettle leaves (see Lyndey's note)
freshly ground black pepper

PICKLE
125 ml (4 fl oz/½ cup) white balsamic or white wine vinegar
115 g (4 oz/½ cup) caster (superfine) sugar
1 small fennel bulb, trimmed and thinly sliced

1 small beetroot (beet), peeled and thinly sliced
3 baby carrots, peeled and thinly sliced
1 fennel sprig with seeds or 1 teaspoon crushed fennel seeds
1 dill sprig with seeds or 1 teaspoon finely chopped dill

ASPARAGUS AND BROAD BEAN SALAD
1 bunch asparagus, trimmed and blanched
75 g (2¾ oz) broad (fava) beans, blanched, with outer skin removed if desired
1 tablespoon lemon juice
1 tablespoon extra-virgin olive oil
salt and freshly ground black pepper

For the pickle, combine the white balsamic vinegar and caster sugar in a small saucepan. Stir over low heat until the sugar dissolves. Increase the heat, bring to the boil and simmer for 2 minutes. Place the sliced fennel, beetroot, carrots, fennel sprig and dill sprig in a heatproof bowl, pour over the balsamic mixture, mix well and set aside.

For the asparagus and broad bean salad, combine all the ingredients and season to taste with salt and pepper.

To cook the pork, heat the olive oil and half the butter in a large frying pan over medium heat. Season the pork steaks with salt to taste, add to the pan and cook for 3 minutes on one side then 2 minutes on the other, or until cooked as desired. Remove to a warm plate, cover with foil and rest.

Return the pan to medium heat, add the wine to deglaze the pan, then add the nettles and simmer to reduce. Add the remaining butter, any pork juices and whisk until the sauce is smooth. Season to taste with salt and pepper.

Serve the pork topped with the sauce, pickle and salad.

When we stayed at beautiful Mt Lofty House in the Adelaide Hills, Girard Ramsay, the executive chef was wonderfully helpful and fed us each night. While not strictly speaking a risotto, this recipe is typical of the innovative food he serves.

QUINOA AND BEETROOT 'RISOTTO', BEETROOT TZATZIKI AND GOAT'S CHEESE

SERVES 4

PREPARATION
20 minutes, plus
3–4 hours for
yoghurt

COOKING 1 hour

WINE
This dish is all about
beetroot, which
matches well with
pinot noir.

500 g (1 lb 2 oz) red beetroots (beets)
  (about 3 medium), washed
1 bunch baby golden beetroots (beets),
  washed
salt
250 g (9 oz/1¼ cups) red quinoa
2 tablespoons extra-virgin olive oil, plus
  extra to serve
4 eschalots, finely chopped
2 garlic cloves, finely chopped
freshly ground black pepper
60 g (2 oz/¼ cup) crème fraîche or light
  sour cream
90 g (3 oz/2 cups) baby English spinach
  leaves

150 g (5½ oz/1 cup) garden peas or broad
  (fava) beans in season
1 cup red sorrel leaves or use the beetroot
  (beet) leaves
50 g (1¾ oz) soft goat's cheese

BEETROOT TZATZIKI
250 g (9 oz/1 cup) natural yoghurt
1 Lebanese (short) cucumber, peeled and
  coarsely grated
1 medium red beetroot (beet), peeled and
  finely grated
1 garlic clove, finely chopped
2 teaspoons lemon juice
salt and freshly ground black pepper

For the beetroot tzatziki, place the yoghurt in a piece of muslin (cheesecloth) in a colander over a bowl and strain in the refrigerator for 3–4 hours, or preferably overnight, to get a thick consistency. Once the yoghurt is ready, place the cucumber into a colander to drain, gently pushing to remove any excess liquid. Combine the yoghurt with the cucumber, beetroot, garlic and lemon juice and season to taste with salt and pepper. Set aside to chill in the refrigerator.

   Bring water to the boil in two medium-sized saucepans. Place the red and golden beetroots in the separate saucepans and cook the golden beetroots for around 40 minutes and the red beetroots for 1 hour, or until you are able to pierce them gently with a paring knife. When cooked, drain and peel the skins off while still warm. Purée two of the red beetroots and cut one into 1 cm (½ in) dice.

»»»

GIRARD'S NOTE

This dish can be a nice vegan main course if you omit the tzatziki, crème fraîche and goat's cheese. You could substitute some olive tapenade or wash the beetroot greens thoroughly and use them instead of the spinach leaves.

Bring a large saucepan of salted water to the boil and cook the quinoa for 15–18 minutes or until soft. Drain and set aside.

Heat 1 tablespoon of the oil over low heat, add the eschalots and garlic and cook, without colouring, until soft. Add the quinoa, and the diced and puréed beetroot and season to taste. Increase the heat to medium and add the crème fraîche, stir together and finally add the spinach and peas and adjust the seasoning.

To serve, spoon the quinoa mixture into a large, deep circular mould or ring (if you have one), level the top, then unmould onto a serving plate. Repeat with the remaining quinoa mixture. Alternatively, use a large crouton cutter on plates, and fill with the quinoa mixture before removing.

Gently reheat the golden beetroots in the remaining oil, spoon around the quinoa, place a spoonful of the tzatziki on top of the quinoa, then scatter with sorrel leaves and place a spoonful of goat's cheese to the side. Drizzle with the extra oil.

If you are intimidated by pastry or are a pastry novice, this olive oil wholemeal (whole-wheat) version is a great place to start. Extra-virgin olive oil and water are simply mixed through flour; no rubbing in of butter is required and no resting before rolling out, either. In fact, I found it best to simply press the dough into an oval shape and flute the edges 'rustically'. I cooked this at the De Bortoli Vineyard in the Yarra Valley using white savourine and goat's curd from Yarra Valley Dairy.

RUSTIC GOAT'S CHEESE TART WITH PINOT ESCHALOTS AND WALNUTS

SERVES 6

PREPARATION
15 minutes

COOKING 1½ hours

WINE

A de Bortoli Yarra Valley pinot noir, of course!

LYNDEY'S NOTE

If the cheese starts to brown too much in the oven, cover the tart with foil for the last 15 minutes.

1 garlic bulb
80 ml (2½ fl oz/⅓ cup) extra-virgin olive oil
15 eschalots (about 500 g/1 lb 2 oz in total), peeled and halved
250 ml (8½ fl oz/1 cup) pinot noir
5 thyme sprigs
salt and freshly ground black pepper
60 g (2 oz/½ cup) pitted black olives
50 g (1¾ oz/½ cup) walnut halves

200 g (7 oz) mature goat's cheese, sliced
120 g (4½ oz/½ cup) goat's curd to serve
55 g (2 oz/¼ cup) caperberries to serve

TART CRUST
320 g (11½ oz/2 cups) wholemeal (whole-wheat) plain (all-purpose) flour
1 teaspoon salt
80 ml (2½ fl oz/⅓ cup) extra-virgin olive oil
125 ml (4 fl oz/½ cup) cold water

Break the garlic bulb open and peel the cloves. Place 2 tablespoons of the oil in a medium deep-sided frying pan with the garlic and eschalots, placed cut side down. Cook over medium heat for 5 minutes or until the eschalots are just starting to colour. Add the pinot noir and thyme, reduce the heat and simmer for 40 minutes, or until the eschalots are tender and the pinot has been absorbed. Season to taste with salt and pepper. Set aside to cool.

Preheat the oven to 200°C (400°F) and line a large baking tray with baking paper.

For the tart crust, combine the flour and salt in a large bowl. Make a well in the centre and add the oil and cold water. Using one hand, quickly mix the ingredients together just until they form a ball. Place the ball on the prepared tray and, using your fingers, push the dough into an oval shape measuring 30 cm x 23 cm (12 in x 9 in). It should be 5 mm (¼ in) thick. Using your thumb and pointer finger, press the pastry edges to form an edge of around 1 cm (½ in). If desired, flute this edge using your fingers.

Top the tart crust with the cooled eschalots, garlic cloves and thyme. Dot with the olives, walnuts and goat's cheese and sprinkle with the remaining oil. Bake for 45 minutes or until the pastry is golden and cooked through.

Serve warm topped with teaspoons of goat's curd and caperberries.

Girard Ramsay from Mt Lofty House in the Adelaide Hills told me about these beautiful local semi-dried plums, so I was determined to use them. They are plump and slightly sticky with a gorgeous concentrated flavour.

SEMI-DRIED PLUM TART WITH CHESTNUT CRUMBLE

SERVES 4

PREPARATION
30 minutes

COOKING
25 minutes

WINE

A sticky or dessert wine from any white grape variety would work well here.

LYNDEY'S NOTE

To make this a totally regional dessert, I used Carême pastry, handmade in the Barossa Valley but any sour cream or shortcrust pastry would work. See Maggie Beer's recipe on page 91. Instead of the plums you could use good-quality prunes. You could use port or topaque instead of muscat.

½ sheet sour cream shortcrust pastry (approximately 25 cm/10 in square) (see Lyndey's note)
3 plums, stoned and quartered, to serve
ground cinnamon to serve

POACHED SEMI-DRIED PLUMS
250 ml (8½ fl oz/1 cup) muscat
2 tablespoons honey
1 bay leaf
1 cinnamon stick
12 semi-dried plums or prunes, halved

CHESTNUT CRUMBLE
100 g (3½ oz) chestnuts, fresh or frozen (defrosted)

45 g (1½ oz/½ cup) flaked almonds
60 g (2 oz) butter
55 g (2 oz/¼ cup) raw (demerara) sugar
35 g (1¼ oz/⅓ cup) ground almonds

CHESTNUT CREAM
50 g (1¾ oz) chestnuts, frozen (defrosted) or fresh in season
2 teaspoons honey
½ teaspoon ground cinnamon, plus extra to dust
100 g (3½ oz) crème fraîche or light sour cream

Cut the pastry into four 12 cm (4¾ in) rounds and place on a tray lined with baking paper. Freeze. For the poached semi-dried plums, combine the muscat, honey, bay leaf and cinnamon stick in a medium saucepan. Bring to the boil, add the plums and simmer for 5 minutes. Remove the plums from the liquid and set aside to cool. Bring the reserved liquid to the boil and simmer until reduced to 80 ml (2½ fl oz/⅓ cup). Discard the bay leaf and cinnamon stick and pour the liquid into a pitcher to serve. For the chestnut crumble, blanch the chestnuts (if fresh) in boiling water for 10 minutes. Peel, drain and cut into small dice. Toast the flaked almonds in a medium frying pan until golden. Remove. To the same frying pan, add the butter, sugar and diced chestnuts. Stir gently over low heat until the butter melts. Increase the heat and continue to cook for 5 minutes or until the chestnuts caramelise. Remove from the heat and stir through the ground almonds and reserved toasted almonds. Preheat the oven to 220°C (430°F). Remove the pastry from the freezer, top each square with six semi-dried plum halves and sprinkle with the chestnut crumble. Bake for 25 minutes or until golden. For the chestnut cream, blanch the chestnuts in boiling water for 10 minutes (if frozen) or 20 (if fresh) or until very soft. Drain then blend or process with the honey and cinnamon until smooth. Stir the chestnut paste through the crème fraîche. Serve each tart with a spoon of chestnut cream dusted with ground cinnamon and the quarters of the three fresh plums drizzled with the reduced poaching liquid.

The extra-virgin olive oil in this cake makes it deliciously moist and saves the effort of having to cream butter. It was ideal to cook outdoors at Abilene Grove in Orange.

PEAR AND VERJUICE SYRUP CAKE

SERVES 12

PREPARATION
10 minutes

COOKING 1 hour

TO DRINK

Tea or coffee is ideal but a sticky dessert wine, like a botrytised semillon or other white grape, suits both the sweetness and fruit in the cake.

LYNDEY'S NOTE

If the pears are really fresh and ripe, there is no need to peel them before adding them to the cake batter. You could reduce pear or apple juice over high heat by half and use instead of the caramelised verjuice.

125 ml (4 fl oz/½ cup) extra-virgin olive oil
2 large eggs
190 ml (6½ fl oz/¾ cup) buttermilk
2 teaspoons vanilla bean paste
300 g (10½ oz/2 cups) self-raising flour
115 g (4 oz/½ cup) caster (superfine) sugar

3 pears, peeled, cored and cut into
  2 cm (¾ in) dice
80 ml (2½ fl oz/⅓ cup) caramelised
  verjuice (see Lyndey's note)
crème fraîche or thick (double/heavy)
  cream to serve

Preheat the oven to 180°C (350°F).

Grease and line the base of a 22 cm (8¾ in) springform cake tin with baking paper.

In a large pitcher, whisk the oil, eggs, buttermilk and vanilla together until well blended. Combine the self-raising flour and caster sugar in a large bowl. Pour the wet mixture over the dry mixture and fold gently until just mixed. Stir through the pears.

Pour into the prepared tin and bake for 1 hour or until the cake is cooked when a skewer inserted in the centre is removed dry with no clinging batter. Cool on a wire rack.

To serve, warm the caramelised verjuice in a small saucepan over low heat or on Low in the microwave and pour over the cooled cake. Serve slices of the cake with crème fraîche or thick cream.

Maggie Beer is a cook, food author, TV personality, restaurateur, businesswoman, food manufacturer and friend. When I was visiting, I asked her to share a dessert recipe with me. She recommends serving this rich tart with her Bitter Oranges in Spiced Verjuice Syrup or candied cumquats. I have developed my own spiced orange recipe here.

MAGGIE BEER'S COFFEE VINCOTTO CHOCOLATE TART WITH BITTER ORANGES

SERVES 6–8

PREPARATION
45 minutes, plus
30 minutes resting,
plus 2 hours cooling

COOKING
25 minutes

WINE
This is an intensely rich hit of chocolate, so a liqueured muscat or topaque works well. But, as a Barossan dish, try a sparkling shiraz.

80 g (2¾ oz) bitter oranges in spiced verjuice syrup (or see below to make your own) or candied cumquats
ice cream to serve (optional)

SOUR CREAM PASTRY
125 g (4½ oz) unsalted butter
160 g (5½ oz) plain (all-purpose) flour
pinch of salt (optional)
60 g (2 oz/¼ cup) sour cream

CHOCOLATE FILLING
200 g (7 oz) dark chocolate 70% cocoa, chopped

100 ml (3½ fl oz) thickened (whipping) cream
15 ml (½ fl oz) strong coffee
15 ml (½ fl oz) vincotto

SPICED ORANGES
125 g (4 oz) sugar
125 ml (4 fl oz/½ cup) verjuice
125 ml (4 fl oz/½ cup) water
1 teaspoon lemon juice
2 small oranges, very thinly sliced in rounds
1 cinnamon stick
1 bay leaf

To make the pastry, dice the butter then pulse with the flour (I like to add a pinch of salt) in a food processor until the mixture resembles fine breadcrumbs. Add the sour cream and continue to pulse until the dough starts to incorporate into a ball. Wrap the dough in plastic wrap and refrigerate for 20–30 minutes before using.

Preheat the oven to 220°C (430°F).

Roll out the pastry on a floured surface or between two sheets of baking paper until thin and large enough to fit into a 36 cm x 13 cm x 2 cm (14½ in x 5 in x ¾ in) greased baking tin. Place the pastry in the tin, trim the edges, top with baking paper and pastry weights and blind bake for 15 minutes. Remove the baking paper and weights and return to the oven for 10 minutes. If the centre of the pastry is still pale and the edges are browning too much, protect the edges by wrapping a length of foil over them. Return to the oven for a further 2 minutes or until golden in the centre. Cool the tart case before filling.

»»»»

LYNDEY'S NOTE

Blind baking prevents the pastry from shrinking and/or rising too much. Although you can buy fancy pastry weights, I just keep a container of rice or dried beans especially for this purpose, and also freeze my pastry in the tin first. Maggie used a 26 cm x 8 cm x 4 cm (10¼ in x 3¼ in x 1½ in) tin when she made hers.

For the chocolate filling, place the chocolate in a medium heatproof bowl. Place the bowl over simmering water, ensuring the water does not touch the base of the bowl or get into the chocolate. Stir gently until melted. Meanwhile, place the cream, coffee and vincotto in a microwave-safe pitcher and microwave on Low for 50 seconds or until warm. Add the warm cream mixture to the melted chocolate and mix until smooth. Pour into the cooled tart and allow to cool at room temperature for 2 hours.

If you are making your own spiced oranges, combine the sugar, verjuice, water and lemon juice in a medium saucepan over low heat and stir until the sugar dissolves. Add the oranges, cinnamon stick and bay leaf and bring to a simmer for 15 minutes. Remove and discard the cinnamon and bay leaf. Remove the oranges and set aside. Bring the syrup to a gentle boil for 5 minutes or until the liquid has reduced and is thick and glossy. Pour the syrup over the oranges and allow to cool until the tart is ready to serve.

When set, arrange the drained spiced oranges on top of the tart. Cut into slices and serve with ice cream, if desired.

This is a delicious grown-up dessert. You could use cherries or berries in place of the rhubarb.

CHOCOLATE, CABERNET AND RHUBARB DESSERT

SERVES 4

PREPARATION
10 minutes

COOKING
10 minutes

WINE
Serve with cabernet sauvignon of course! The chocolatey character of cabernet marries well with this dish, and the wine has enough power for its intensity of flavour.

500 ml (17 fl oz/2 cups) cabernet sauvignon
110 g (4 oz/½ cup) caster (superfine) sugar, plus 1 tablespoon extra
1 small cinnamon stick
2 cloves
2 star anise

1 bunch rhubarb (5 stalks), washed
75 ml (2½ fl oz) pouring (single/light) cream
75 g (2¾ oz) chocolate, broken up
1 teaspoon vanilla bean paste
300 g (10½ oz) crème fraîche or light sour cream

Place the wine, the 110 g (4 oz/½ cup) of caster sugar and the spices in a large saucepan over medium heat. Stir until the sugar is dissolved.

Cut the rhubarb into lengths, add it to the simmering cabernet syrup and move it around very gently with a wooden spoon. When just tender, remove the rhubarb to a bowl.

Increase the heat under the cabernet syrup and simmer until thickened and reduced to 125 ml (4 fl oz/½ cup). Strain, pour over the rhubarb and allow to cool.

Meanwhile put the cream and chocolate in a saucepan over low heat. Melt the chocolate and stir to combine. (Alternatively do this in a microwave on Low for a couple of minutes.) Cool but do not chill.

Gently fold the vanilla and the extra tablespoon of sugar, through the crème fraîche.

Spread a quarter of the crème fraîche mixture onto each serving dish, top with rhubarb pieces and drizzle with some syrup. Top with the chocolate and serve immediately.

Everyone loves a brownie but I wanted the honey to be hero when I cooked a blondie instead at the historic Beekeeper's Inn near Orange.

LUSCIOUS HONEY BLONDIES

MAKES 24

PREPARATION
10 minutes

COOKING
35 minutes

125 g (4½ oz) butter
100 g (3½ oz) white chocolate, broken into pieces
115 g (4 oz/½ cup) firmly packed brown sugar
90 g (3 oz/¼ cup) honey

1 teaspoon vanilla bean paste
100 g (3½ oz/⅔ cup) self-raising flour
½ teaspoon salt
2 eggs, lightly beaten
50 g (1¾ oz) dark chocolate, melted
50 g (1¾ oz) white chocolate, melted

WINE

For a change, try an oloroso sherry, which is semi-sweet yet powerful enough for the chocolate.

Preheat the oven to 180°C (350°F) and line the base and sides of a 20 cm x 20 cm (8 in x 8 in) baking dish with baking paper.

Melt the butter, white chocolate pieces, brown sugar and honey in a medium saucepan over medium heat, stirring until smooth. Remove from the heat, add the vanilla, flour, salt and eggs and mix with a wooden spoon until combined. Pour into the prepared tin and bake for 30 minutes or until just firm. Cool on a wire rack.

Cut the blondies into bars, place on a serving platter and drizzle with the melted dark chocolate and then the melted white chocolate. Leave to set for a few minutes before serving.

This recipe was contributed by Yarra Valley Dairy. Their cheeses are fantastic and the Black Savourine is a semi-matured, ashed goat's cheese that has a creamy, slightly acidic, taste.

BLACK SAVOURINE WITH CARDAMOM ROASTED PLUMS AND FRUIT BREAD

SERVES 4

PREPARATION
10 minutes

COOKING
20–30 minutes

WINE

This dish is not overly sweet, so choose a late-picked riesling rather than a botrytised wine.

6 firm plums (about 675 g/1½ lb), halved and stoned
55 g (2 oz/¼ cup) firmly packed brown sugar
60 ml (2 fl oz/¼ cup) orange juice

4 cardamom pods, bruised
200 g (7 oz) Yarra Valley Dairy Black Savourine or other semi-matured ashed goat's cheese
thinly sliced fruit bread for serving

Preheat the oven to 200°C (400°F).

Place the plums, cut side down, in a single layer in a shallow baking dish. Sprinkle with the sugar and orange juice and dot with cardamom pods. Bake for 20–30 minutes or until the plums are soft and tender – this will vary depending on the ripeness of the plums. Once cooked, remove from the oven and take the plums out of the baking dish so that they do not continue to cook. Allow to cool.

Serve the cardamom roasted plums with the Yarra Valley Dairy Black Savourine and thinly sliced fruit bread.

THE
WATER
WAYS

Lyndey with Sean Blocksidge of the Margaret
River Discovery Company, canoeing on the
Margaret River, Western Australia.

Australia is an island nation with more than 10,000 beaches, including some of the most
magnificent in the world. It's also one of the most urbanised and coast-dwelling nations
with more than 80 per cent of Australians living within 100 kilometres (62 miles) of the
coast. No wonder Australia has a reputation as a water-loving country!

The Shoalhaven region on the south coast of New South Wales is a majestic stretch of
coastline endowed with beaches, bays, rivers, national parks like Jervis Bay National Park,
historic country towns and natural attractions.

The biggest champion of the area is international chef, author and TV presenter Rick
Stein. He has the award-winning restaurant Rick Stein at Bannisters in Mollymook. This
coastal cliff-top hideaway is in a boutique hotel, also with poolside cocktail and pizza bar.
It reminds Rick of his home in Cornwall and, once he met the local fishmonger, Lucky,
he knew he could do well there. According to Rick, 'to say this comes from somewhere
specific ... it just gives people a little, sort of, emotional tie to that food ... And you say
something like Clyde River oysters ... or Illawarra prawns, you think, "Oh, where is it?
Where is the Clyde River? What's so special about them?"' So it was very special to forage
for seaweed and periwinkles with Rick himself, who's been a friend for 17 years.

Sydney rock oysters (the name of the species not the location) are grown in innovative
floating baskets along the Clyde River, while further up the Clyde River Berry Farm offers
pick-your-own blueberries, boysenberries, loganberries, youngberries and tayberries – all
of which are derived from raspberries and blackberries. There are local providores and an
increasing number of wineries.

Inland, Bundanon Homestead and Arthur Boyd's Studio – this significant artist's gift to the nation because 'you can't own a landscape' – is open every Sunday. Best of all, kangaroos come down to feed before dusk on Pebbly Beach where, like me, you can get the holiday photo of a lifetime.

Jervis Bay, nearly 200 kilometres (124 miles) south of Sydney, has the whitest fine sand in the world and is home to between 80 and 130 bottlenose dolphins, so you're pretty sure to get a sighting if you take a cruise out from Huskisson. Whales can be sighted from mid-May to late November and swim all the way up the coast.

Whale sightings are also popular at Port Macquarie in northern New South Wales where the town green is beside the dazzling waterway. Here the maritime climate means that seafood, tomatoes, macadamia nuts and more vineyards flourish. You can ride a camel on the beach or visit The Port Macquarie Koala Hospital – for over 40 years the only hospital in the world dedicated to the preservation, conservation and care of wild koalas.

However it's not all beaches – there are also beautiful lakes and rivers throughout Australia. The Hawkesbury and its tributary, the Nepean River, virtually encircle the metropolitan region of Sydney. The Hawkesbury wends its way west and north of Sydney for 120 kilometres (75 miles) and is known for the lush fertile farming land on its banks. Near Ebenezer, Melanda Park – which previously farmed cattle, kale, citrus and potatoes – is now home to some very happy – and hungry – free-range pigs. Australian pigs are said to be the most ethically raised in the world and here I learned that in Australia we're not allowed to feed pigs swill (restaurant or kitchen waste or anything that contains meat) but only fruit, vegetables and plants.

OK, so this is not strictly a carbonara sauce, but then calamari isn't pasta either. This is delightfully gluten-free, using calamari in place of pasta – an idea I got from a restaurant in Paris – isn't Australia delightfully multicultural? It does need some cream because the calamari itself is not enough to 'cook' the egg yolks as in the case of a real carbonara.

CALAMARI ALLA CARBONARA

SERVES 4

PREPARATION
10 minutes (longer if you clean your own calamari)

COOKING 6 minutes

WINE

The round, rich flavours of the sauce demand a round, rich wine like a chardonnay or even a viognier.

150 g (5½ oz) good-quality bacon (about 2 thick rashers/slices), cut into lardons
2 garlic cloves
300 ml (10 fl oz) pouring (single/light) cream
400 g (14 oz) cleaned calamari (about 500 g/1 lb 2 oz whole squid or 2 whole tubes)

1 tablespoon extra-virgin olive oil
salt and freshly ground black pepper to taste
½ bunch chives, chopped
4 egg yolks
25 g (1 oz/¼ cup) freshly grated parmesan

Dry-fry the bacon in a small frying pan over medium heat until crisp. Remove two-thirds of the bacon and reserve for garnish. Pour off any excess fat. Add the garlic cloves and cream to the remaining bacon in the pan and simmer until thickened and sauce-like. Strain, discard the bacon and garlic and keep warm.

Open out the calamari tubes and cut into 5 mm (¼ in) strips then toss in a bowl with the oil and salt to taste.

Preheat a large frying pan over high heat and cook the calamari for only a couple of minutes, tossing frequently. Reduce the heat and stir through a generous grinding of black pepper, the warm bacon and garlic cream sauce and the chives.

Divide between four warm bowls. Make a well in the centre of each bowl, slide in an egg yolk, sprinkle with the reserved bacon, grated parmesan and more black pepper and serve immediately.

Moqueca is a Brazilian coconut milk-based stew, mildly flavoured with chilli and sweet paprika. Normally only white fish is used, but I've added crab, mussels and clams for variety. Serve with steamed quinoa or rice to mop up the flavoursome sauce.

MOQUECA WITH CRAB, MUSSELS AND CLAMS

SERVES 4

PREPARATION
25 minutes

COOKING
18 minutes

WINE

This naturally goes with wine styles that do well in the South American continent, like sauvignon blanc or malbec. There is a synergy in the flavours and it works equally well, though differently, with white or red grapes.

LYNDEY'S NOTE

You can replace the stock with extra coconut milk, if desired.

60 ml (2 fl oz/¼ cup) extra-virgin olive oil
1 brown onion, finely chopped
1 small red capsicum (bell pepper), finely chopped
1 small yellow capsicum (bell pepper), finely chopped
4 garlic cloves, finely chopped
3 teaspoons sweet paprika
1 bay leaf
½ teaspoon dried red chilli flakes
250 g (9 oz) cherry or grape tomatoes, halved

405 ml (13½ fl oz/1⅔ cups) coconut milk
250 ml (8½ fl oz/1 cup) fish or chicken stock
2 x 350 g (12½ oz) blue swimmer crabs
300 g (10½ oz) firm white fish fillets, such as ling or blue eye trevalla, cut into 4 cm (1½ in) dice
500 g (1 lb 2 oz) mussels, debearded
400 g (14 oz) clams, rinsed and drained
salt and freshly ground black pepper to taste
coriander (cilantro) leaves to serve

Heat the oil in a large deep frying pan with a lid. Add the onion and red and yellow capsicum and cook for 5 minutes or until softened. Add the garlic, paprika, bay leaf, chilli flakes and tomatoes and cook for a further 5 minutes. Add the coconut milk and stock, bring to the boil and simmer for 5 minutes.

Prepare the crabs by lifting the flap under the body and pulling off and discarding the top shell. Remove and discard the gills – also known as dead man's fingers. Cut each crab into quarters.

Add the crab, fish, mussels and clams to the moqueca, then cover and cook for 2–3 minutes or until the crab flesh is white and the mussels and clams have opened. Discard any mussels or clams that do not open. Season to taste with salt and pepper and serve topped with coriander leaves.

LINGUINE WITH SEAFOOD AND GARLIC CRUMBS

SERVES 4

PREPARATION
15 minutes

COOKING
15 minutes

WINE

This dish celebrates fresh seafood and the wine needs to enhance that, so go for the delicate flavours of a semillon – one with a little age will develop toasty flavours and also work with the crumb.

LYNDEY'S NOTE

If you twist the bowl as you place the linguine down, the pasta will swirl into a very neat pile.

80 ml (2½ fl oz/⅓ cup) extra-virgin olive oil
1 kg (2 lb 3 oz) mixed seafood – john dory fillets, scallops and mussels, debearded
2 baby fennel bulbs (about 260 g/9 oz), thinly sliced, fronds reserved
2 garlic cloves, finely chopped
2 zucchini (courgettes), cut into thin matchsticks
250 g (9 oz) cherry tomatoes, halved or 2 medium tomatoes, peeled, seeded and chopped
60 ml (2 fl oz/¼ cup) dry white wine

salt and freshly ground black pepper to taste
500 g (1 lb 2 oz) linguine
1 bunch chives, finely chopped

GARLIC CRUMBS
60 ml (2 fl oz/¼ cup) extra-virgin olive oil
1 large red chilli, finely chopped
1 large green chilli, finely chopped
1 garlic clove, finely chopped
70 g (2½ oz/1 cup) fresh sourdough breadcrumbs

Make the garlic crumbs by heating the oil in a large non-stick frying pan. Add the chilli, garlic and breadcrumbs and cook, stirring, for a few minutes or until crisp. Remove from the pan and reserve.

For the seafood, heat half the oil in a large frying pan over medium heat and sear the john dory fillets and scallops on both sides until almost cooked. Remove from the pan to a warm place and reserve.

Add the remaining oil to the pan and cook the fennel until it is beginning to soften. Add the garlic and zucchini and cook for 1 minute more, stirring until fragrant. Add the tomatoes, wine and mussels and simmer, covered, until hot and the mussels open. Discard any mussels that do not open. Season to taste with salt and pepper.

Meanwhile cook the linguine in a large saucepan of boiling salted water following the packet instructions; drain, reserving 125 ml (4 fl oz/½ cup) of the cooking liquid.

Add the fennel fronds and chives to the mussels and vegetables, then add the drained pasta. Toss gently, adding the reserved cooking liquid if necessary. Serve topped with the john dory, scallops and garlic crumbs.

One of the highlights of filming Taste of Australia *was foraging and cooking with my long-time friend Rick Stein at his restaurant and hotel Bannisters at Mollymook on the New South Wales south coast. He cooked this on a barbecue overlooking the ocean, but of course it could easily be cooked in a frying pan.*

SNAPPER WITH MANGO SALSA

SERVES 4

PREPARATION
10 minutes

COOKING
10 minutes

WINE
The fresh, light and limey flavours here cry out for the same in a riesling or semillon – and both can handle chilli.

LYNDEY'S NOTE
Coila prawns are so named because they come from Coila Lake near Tuross on the south coast of New South Wales. Dutch chillies are long, slender and pointed and not as fiery as some. You could use any other type of chilli, if you can't find the Dutch variety.

4 x 175 g (6 oz) pieces snapper, skin on
extra-virgin olive oil to brush and serve
salt and freshly ground black pepper
    to taste

MANGO SALSA
100 g (3½ oz) cooked, peeled Coila
    prawns (shrimp) (about 4 medium
    prawns) or peeled, cooked yabbies
1 ripe but firm mango, peeled and cut
    into 1 cm (½ in) dice

1 ripe but firm avocado, peeled and
    cut into 1 cm (½ in) dice
4 spring onions (scallions), thinly sliced
2 large medium–hot red Dutch chillies,
    seeded and thinly sliced
2 finger limes, seeds scraped out
juice of ½ lime
2 tablespoons extra-virgin olive oil
1 handful of baby coriander (cilantro)
    leaves
salt and freshly ground black pepper
    to taste

Preheat a barbecue to high.

Brush both sides of the snapper fillets with the oil and season with salt and pepper. Cook the fillets on the barbecue, skin side down, for 3–5 minutes. Turn the snapper and cook for a further 3–5 minutes or until just cooked through.

Cut the prawns or yabbies into small chunks and mix gently in a large bowl with the remaining salsa ingredients, reserving a few finger lime seeds for garnish. Season to taste with salt and pepper.

To serve, divide the salsa among four serving plates and top each with a piece of snapper. Drizzle with a little oil, sprinkle with some extra salt and garnish with a few finger lime pearls.

Although this slaw is not strictly Portuguese in influence, it goes really well with Piri piri spatchcock (page 115), as does the corn, which mirrors the spiced flavours of the piri piri.

SPICED CORN WITH RED CABBAGE SLAW

SERVES 4

PREPARATION
15 minutes

COOKING
15 minutes

WINE

If eating this with the Piri piri spatchcock, stick with the gewürztraminer or dolcetto recommended for that recipe, which work well with these flavours, too.

4 whole corn cobs with husks and silks

SPICED BUTTER
2 teaspoons sweet paprika
2 teaspoons dried thyme
2 teaspoons mustard powder
1/2 teaspoon cayenne pepper
1 teaspoon white pepper
1 teaspoon salt
40 g (1½ oz) butter, melted

RED CABBAGE SLAW
60 g (2 oz/½ cup) slivered almonds, toasted
¼ small red cabbage, shredded
1 small carrot, grated
4 spring onions (scallions), sliced
4 radishes, cut into thin matchsticks
125 ml (4 fl oz/½ cup) buttermilk
1 tablespoon apple cider vinegar
2 teaspoons maple syrup
1 tablespoon poppy seeds
salt and freshly ground black pepper to taste

Preheat a barbecue to hot.

Carefully roll back the corn husks (but do not remove them) and remove the silk. Soak the corn cobs with their husks in water while you prepare the spiced butter.

Combine the spiced butter ingredients in a small bowl. Drain the corn and brush with the spiced butter. Carefully pull the husks back over the cob, keeping the butter in place, to prevent them from burning. Place on the barbecue and reduce the heat to medium–high. Cook for 15 minutes or until tender, turning several times to cook evenly. Pull the hood down if you have a hooded barbecue. (Alternatively you can roast in a 200°C/400°F oven for 15 minutes.)

For the red cabbage slaw, combine the almonds, cabbage, carrot, spring onion and radishes in a medium bowl. Whisk together the buttermilk, vinegar, maple syrup and poppy seeds in a small bowl. Season to taste with salt and pepper, pour over the cabbage mixture then serve with the spiced corn.

It is thought that the Portuguese introduced the chilli to Europe and the Far East. Piri piri is a traditional Portuguese chilli sauce, which is very popular in Australia and easy to make at home. I like to serve this with the Spiced corn with red cabbage slaw (page 113).

PIRI PIRI SPATCHCOCK

SERVES 4

PREPARATION
20 minutes, plus
3 hours marinating

COOKING
20 minutes, plus
resting

WINE

This dish is quite hot and spicy so a wine with some sweetness is called for. For white wine, try a gewürztraminer. For red, try a dolcetto – the name means 'little sweet one' in Italian.

4 x 500 g (1 lb 2 oz) whole free-range spatchcocks (Cornish game hens)
1 teaspoon salt
2 tablespoons flat-leaf (Italian) parsley, roughly chopped

PIRI PIRI MARINADE
80 ml (2½ fl oz/⅓ cup) extra-virgin olive oil
4 bird's eye chillies, chopped
6 garlic cloves, peeled and chopped
1½ tablespoons sweet paprika
2 teaspoons ground coriander
1 teaspoon ground cumin
1 teaspoon ground cinnamon
1 teaspoon ground ginger
2 tablespoons white wine vinegar or lemon juice

For the piri piri marinade, warm 1 tablespoon of the oil in a small saucepan over medium–low heat and cook the chillies, garlic, spices and ginger gently until aromatic. Process in a small blender with the remaining oil and the vinegar until it forms a paste. Allow to cool.

To butterfly each spatchcock, place it, breast side down, on a board. Using kitchen scissors, cut along each side of the backbone and remove. Discard or save for stock. Turn the spatchcock over with the legs pointing outwards and wings pointing down towards the legs then flatten with your hands.

Gently push your fingers between the skin and breast of each spatchcock. Divide the piri piri marinade into quarters. Push most of each quarter under the skin of each spatchcock and spread the remainder on the legs and thighs. Cover and refrigerate for at least 3 hours to marinate if possible.

Preheat a barbecue to medium heat and place a silicone sheet, piece of foil or baking paper on the flat hotplate. Season the spatchcocks with the salt and place them, breast side up, on the foil. Cover and cook for 20 minutes or until the juices run clear when the thigh is pierced with a skewer.

Remove the spatchcocks from the oven, cover loosely with foil and allow to rest for 5–10 minutes. Scatter with the parsley and serve.

This is a foolproof method of cooking pork and keeping it moist, called 6–2–2. First you cook the pork for 6 minutes on one side, then 2 minutes on the other, then rest for 2 minutes. Easy! I cooked this at beautiful Melanda Park on the Hawkesbury River in New South Wales.

THE PERFECT PORK STEAK WITH FIGS AND SOFT POLENTA

SERVES 4

PREPARATION
10 minutes

COOKING
10 minutes, plus
2 minutes resting

WINE
Pinot gris, viognier or chardonnay all work well in different ways with the creamy polenta, juicy pork and luscious figs.

LYNDEY'S NOTE
It is important not to flip the steak when removing it from the pan to rest as the juices will have risen to the top and the steak will dry out if flipped. If you prefer a 'hint of pink', then reduce cooking times accordingly.

2 tablespoons extra-virgin olive oil
8 sage leaves
4 x 180 g (6½ oz) pork steaks, cut
  2 cm (¾ in) thick
salt and freshly ground black pepper
  to taste
4 figs, halved or quartered if large
1 tablespoon wholegrain mustard
100 ml (3½ fl oz) verjuice
80 g (2¾ oz) pancetta (about 4 slices),
  chopped
2 garlic cloves, finely chopped
2 tablespoons pine nuts

1 bunch cavolo nero (Tuscan cabbage),
  trimmed
125 ml (4 fl oz/½ cup) chicken stock
  or water

POLENTA
375 ml (12½ fl oz/1½ cups) chicken stock
375 ml (12½ fl oz/1½ cups) water
250 g (9 oz/1½ cups) instant polenta
250 ml (8½ fl oz/1 cup) milk
20 g (¾ oz) butter
salt and freshly ground black pepper
  to taste

For the polenta, combine the stock and water in a medium saucepan and bring to the boil. Gradually whisk in the polenta. Continue to whisk and pour in the milk. Cook over low heat, stirring occasionally, until the liquid is absorbed and the polenta is tender, around 5 minutes. Stir in the butter and season to taste with salt and pepper. Set aside and whisk occasionally, while preparing the pork.

Meanwhile for the pork, heat 1 tablespoon of the oil in a large frying pan over medium–high heat. Fry the sage leaves until crisp, drain on paper towel and set aside until serving. Season the pork steaks on both sides with salt and pepper. Place in the frying pan and cook on one side only for 6 minutes. Turn and cook on the other side for a further 2 minutes. Remove to a plate without flipping (see Lyndey's note), cover loosely with foil and rest for 2 minutes. Add the figs to the pan, increase the heat to high, add the mustard and verjuice and bring to the boil. Add any juices from the resting pork plate.

While the pork rests, heat the remaining 1 tablespoon oil in a large frying pan, add the pancetta, garlic and pine nuts and cook, stirring, until the pancetta is golden and the nuts are lightly browned. Add the cavolo nero and stock or water and cook, stirring, until wilted.

To serve, place a large spoonful of polenta on each plate and top with the pork, figs in sauce from the pan, reserved crisp sage leaves and cavolo nero on the side.

The key to good pork crackling is a good layer of fat under dry skin, so ideally begin this recipe the day before. Score the skin (or ask your butcher to do this) then place the pork, uncovered, in the refrigerator overnight to ensure the skin is dry and then be sure to rub salt well into the skin and the cuts between it. If all else fails, you can take the crackling off and crisp it up under a hot grill (broiler) or even in the microwave (see Lyndey's note).

ROAST PORK, WINTER VEG AND SAVOURY APPLE CRUMBLE

SERVES 8

PREPARATION
30 minutes,
plus overnight
refrigeration for
'drying' the skin

COOKING 1 hour
35 minutes, plus
20 minutes resting

WINE
With all the wonderful
flavour and texture
going on here, try a
pinot gris.

2 kg (4 lb 6 oz) boneless pork loin
sea salt
2 kg (4 lb 6 oz) parsnips, peeled
800 g (1 lb 12 oz) sweet potato, peeled
    and cut into 3 cm (1¼ in) chunks
2 tablespoons extra-virgin olive oil
freshly ground black pepper to taste
125 ml (4 fl oz/½ cup) apple cider
500 ml (17 fl oz/2 cups) chicken stock
4 bunches broccolini, steamed, to serve

SAVOURY APPLE CRUMBLE
60 g (2 oz) butter
1 small brown onion, finely chopped
1 small fennel bulb, finely chopped
1 teaspoon fennel seeds
70 g (2½ oz/½ cup) hazelnuts, roughly
    chopped
1 tablespoon finely chopped sage
70 g (2½ oz/1 cup) fresh sourdough
    breadcrumbs
2 small, firm tart apples, cored and
    thinly sliced
salt and freshly ground black pepper
    to taste

To prepare the pork, score the skin by making cuts 1 cm (½ in) apart using a very sharp knife or Stanley (craft) knife. Even if your butcher has done this for you, it is often wise to add extra scores. Place the pork in a colander or on a wire rack in the sink and pour over a kettle full of boiling water. Dry the skin very well with paper towel then place in the refrigerator for a couple of hours or preferably overnight.

    Remove the pork from the refrigerator and check that the rind is dry and, if desired, use a hairdryer on the cold setting to ensure it is. Rub generously with salt, massaging it into the cuts in the skin. Leave at room temperature while the oven preheats to 230°C (445°F). Place the pork on a wire rack in a heavy baking dish and roast for around 30 minutes or until the skin begins to crackle.

»»»

LYNDEY'S NOTE

Pumpkin (winter squash) can be used in place of the sweet potato. To crisp crackling in the microwave, put it on a couple of layers of paper towel, cover loosely with another couple of layers and microwave on High for 1–2 minutes. It will become crunchy as it cools. Repeat if the crackling is still not crunchy enough.

Meanwhile, line a large baking tray with baking paper. Cut the parsnips into chunks and remove the centre if woody. Place on the baking tray with the sweet potato, drizzle with oil and season with salt and pepper.

If the skin goes all the way round the pork including underneath, turn the pork over after 30 minutes so the other side will become crisp. (Insert a meat thermometer if you have one.) Reduce the oven temperature to 190°C (375°F), place the sweet potatoes and parsnips in the oven and continue to cook for 30 minutes.

To make the crumble, melt the butter in a medium saucepan. Add the onion, fennel, fennel seeds and hazelnuts and cook for 10 minutes or until the onion and fennel are soft. Add the sage, breadcrumbs and apple, season with salt and pepper and mix well. Spoon into a baking dish.

If you turned the pork over to crisp the skin underneath, turn it over again. Increase the heat to 230°C (445°F) and cook for a further 15 minutes. Test for doneness with the meat thermometer (the internal temperature should be 63–70°C/145–158°F for medium and 72–75°C/162–167°F for well done), or until the juices run clear. Remove the pork to a warm plate, cover loosely with foil and rest for 20 minutes. Place the crumble in the oven, reduce the heat to 200°C (400°F) and leave the crumble and veg in to cook for 20 minutes while the pork rests.

Pour out any excess fat from the pork baking dish, place over high heat on the stove and add the apple cider and chicken stock. Bring to the boil, scraping the base of the baking dish to dislodge the sediment. Reduce the liquid by about half. Season to taste with salt and pepper.

To serve, carve the pork into slices, drizzle with the cider jus and serve with the crumble, winter veg and broccolini.

The azure waters of the New South Wales south coast are home to pods of playful dolphins.

When I visited artist Arthur Boyd's property, Bundanon, the education officer, Saskia Vrenegoor, brought me some stinging nettles. I always marvel that their sting disappears as soon as they are cooked. This recipe takes inspiration from the adjacent cattle farm and landscape.

SPICED RIB EYE WITH QUINOA AND STINGING NETTLE SALAD

SERVES 4

PREPARATION
15 minutes

COOKING
25 minutes, plus resting

WINE

Beef and spices demand a shiraz! I matched this dish with a Southern Highlands syrah from my friend Rosie Cupitt.

2 x 600 g (1 lb 5 oz) beef rib eye steaks, on the bone
2 teaspoons ground coriander
3 teaspoons ground cumin
salt and freshly ground black pepper
125 g (4½ oz/½ cup) thick Greek-style yoghurt
1 tablespoon extra-virgin olive oil

NETTLE AND GRAIN SALAD
200 g (7 oz/1 cup) quinoa
1 cup stinging nettles (or baby rocket/arugula)
1 bunch coriander (cilantro), leaves roughly chopped
1 bunch flat-leaf (Italian) parsley, leaves roughly chopped

1 bunch mint, leaves roughly chopped
1 eschalot, thinly sliced
2 tablespoons pepitas (pumpkin seeds), toasted
2 tablespoons slivered almonds, toasted
2 tablespoons pine nuts, toasted
75 g (2¾ oz) currants or sultanas (golden raisins)
seeds of 1 pomegranate (optional)
salt and freshly ground black pepper to taste
juice and finely grated zest of 1 lemon
60 ml (2 fl oz/¼ cup) extra-virgin olive oil

LYNDEY'S NOTE

To remove the seeds from a pomegranate, slice the fruit in half then turn and bash with the back of a wooden spoon over a small bowl.

For the nettle and grain salad, rinse the quinoa in water, drain and toast it in a small saucepan for a few minutes, stirring frequently. Add 500 ml (17 fl oz/2 cups) water and cook according to the packet directions. Cover and cook over low heat until tender, approximately 15 minutes. In the last couple of minutes of cooking, add the stinging nettles, and cook, stirring until wilted. Remove from the heat and set aside to cool.

Rub the steaks with the ground coriander and 2 teaspoons of the cumin and season to taste. Set aside to absorb the flavours. Combine the remaining cumin with the yoghurt.

Mix the remaining salad ingredients, except the lemon juice and zest and oil, together in a large bowl. Add the quinoa and nettle mixture and season to taste with salt and pepper. Whisk together the lemon juice and zest and oil and dress the salad just prior to serving.

Heat a large frying pan over high heat and add the oil. Add the beef and cook for 5 minutes or until brown and crusted on one side. Turn and cover with a lid or foil and cook for a further 5 minutes or until brown, crusted and cooked as desired. Remove to a warm plate and cover loosely with foil to rest for 5–10 minutes.

To serve, carve the meat off the bones and then slice downwards to make thin slices. Divide the salad among four serving plates, surround with steak and top with the combined yoghurt and cumin.

The beautiful berries I collected from Clyde River Berry Farm and the walnuts in honey from Carole Ruta of South Coast Providores in Berry were taken to the next level with a local dessert wine, Two Figs Sticky Fig. I used layers of blueberries, marionberries and boysenberries but you could use any berries you liked, such as boysenberries, raspberries or strawberries. This is a great dessert for a crowd.

VERY BERRY TRIFLE

SERVES 12

PREPARATION
20 minutes, plus at least 1 hour refrigeration

COOKING
10 minutes

WINE

For a perfect match, drink the same dessert wine you use to soften the savoiardi.

approximately 250 g (9 oz) savoiardi (lady fingers)
125 ml (4 fl oz/½ cup) dessert wine
500 g (1 lb 2 oz) each blueberries, raspberries and boysenberries
½ cup walnuts in honey (or ¼ cup toasted walnut halves plus 175 g/6 oz/½ cup honey)
fresh blackcurrants to garnish (optional)

SABAYON
6 egg yolks
80 g (2¾ oz/⅓ cup) caster (superfine) sugar
190 ml (6½ fl oz/¾ cup) sparkling white wine
300 ml (10 fl oz) thickened (whipping) cream, firmly whipped

To make the sabayon, whisk the egg yolks and caster sugar in a medium bowl until pale. Place over a saucepan of simmering water and gradually whisk in the sparkling wine until the mixture thickens and coats the back of a spoon. Don't rush this — it will take 5–10 minutes. Remove from the heat and cool, whisking occasionally. (Ideally whisk over a bowl of ice until cold.) When cold, fold through the whipped cream.

Place a third of the savoiardi in the base of a large glass bowl of 3 litre (101 fl oz/ 12 cup) capacity. Drizzle with a couple of tablespoons of the dessert wine. Spoon a third of the sabayon over the sponge. Layer the blueberries on top. Layer another third of the savoiardi on top, drizzle with half the remaining dessert wine, then another third of the sabayon, then a layer of marionberries; then the last third of the savoiardi, the remaining dessert wine, sabayon and finishing with boysenberries. Alternatively, you can put a combination of berries in each layer. Spoon over the walnuts in honey.

Cover and refrigerate for at least an hour or overnight for the flavours to meld and the savoiardi to soften.

The perennially popular cheesecake is given a modern update with no biscuit (cookie) base, but rather a moreish praline made with macadamia nuts from Lorne Valley, south-west of Port Macquarie, New South Wales. I cooked the dish overlooking the beach on a wild and woolly afternoon.

UPSIDE DOWN SALTED CARAMEL CHEESECAKE WITH MACADAMIA PRALINE

SERVES 4

PREPARATION
15 minutes, plus cooling time

COOKING
20 minutes

WINE
Rather than a dessert wine, try the luscious flavours of an oloroso sherry.

LYNDEY'S NOTE
This dessert can be made ahead and refrigerated (without the praline), but for best results, remove from the refrigerator at least 1 hour before serving sprinkled with the praline.

125 ml (4 fl oz/½ cup) pouring (single/ light) cream
185 g (6½ oz/¾ cup) cream cheese, softened
1 teaspoon vanilla bean paste

SALTED CARAMEL SAUCE
60 g (2 oz) butter
110 g (4 oz/½ cup) muscovado or dark brown sugar
125 ml (4 fl oz/½ cup) pouring (single/ light) cream

1 teaspoon sea salt flakes
1 teaspoon vanilla bean paste

MACADAMIA PRETZEL PRALINE
40 g (1½ oz) butter
2 tablespoons maple syrup
55 g (2 oz/⅓ cup) icing (confectioners') sugar
70 g (2½ oz/½ cup) macadamia nuts, toasted and roughly chopped
½ cup roughly crushed pretzels

For the salted caramel sauce, melt the butter in a medium saucepan, add the sugar and cook for 5 minutes or until the sugar dissolves and starts to turn golden, stirring from time to time. Add the cream and salt and bring to the boil. Boil gently for 10 minutes, whisking occasionally, until thickened. Remove from the heat and pour into a small bowl; add the vanilla and set aside to cool.

For the macadamia pretzel praline, place a medium saucepan over low heat, add the butter and melt, stirring from time to time to distribute the milk solids and continue to cook until it foams and turns nut brown. Stir in the maple syrup and icing sugar, bring to the boil and cook for 2 minutes. Add the macadamia nuts and crushed pretzels and stir quickly until coated. Spoon onto a baking tray lined with baking paper and set aside to cool. When cool, break into small chunks.

Using an electric mixer, beat the cream until soft peaks form. In a larger bowl, using the same beaters, whip the cream cheese, vanilla and 1 tablespoon of the cooled salted caramel sauce until fluffy. Gently fold through the cream.

Spoon into serving glasses, top with a spoonful of salted caramel sauce and scatter over a few chunks of macadamia pretzel praline. Serve immediately.

My long-time friend Carole Ruta from South Coast Providores in Berry gave me this recipe. She told me, 'This is based on an old English recipe of my mother's which traditionally used raspberry conserve. As rhubarb is abundant in south coast gardens we prefer to use it instead. So simple, but impressive.'

RHUBARB QUEEN OF PUDDINGS

SERVES 6

PREPARATION
30 minutes

COOKING
45 minutes

WINE

The honeyed flavours of a botrytis wine will reflect the honey in the pudding.

LYNDEY'S NOTE

Good-quality rhubarb conserve can be substituted for the roasted rhubarb.

300 ml (10 fl oz) milk
300 ml (10 fl oz) pouring (single/light) cream
1 vanilla bean, split lengthways
4 eggs, separated
125 g (4½ oz) crushed savoiardi (lady fingers)
145 g (5 oz/⅔ cup) caster (superfine) sugar

ROASTED RHUBARB

1 bunch rhubarb, leaves removed, washed and cut into 2 cm (¾ in) pieces
90 g (3 oz/¼ cup) honey

Preheat the oven to 180°C (350°F).

Bring the milk, cream and vanilla bean to the boil in a medium saucepan. Remove from the heat and set aside for 20 minutes.

For the roasted rhubarb, place the rhubarb on a baking tray lined with baking paper, drizzle with the honey and bake for 15 minutes or until tender.

Whisk the egg yolks and slowly add the milk mixture, discarding the vanilla bean. Stir in the savoiardi crumbs. Divide between six 250 ml (8½ fl oz/1 cup) ovenproof ramekins or moulds and bake for 15 minutes.

For the meringue, whisk the egg whites until soft peaks form and gradually add the sugar, whisking until the mixture is glossy.

Remove the puddings from the oven and top with the roasted rhubarb. Divide the meringue on top of the puddings and use a knife or fork to create peaks. Return to the oven and bake for a further 15 minutes. Serve immediately.

Joanne Scott, who runs Lorne Valley Macadamia Farm with her husband, Ray, also runs a café on site. This cake is very popular with her customers.

CARROT AND MACADAMIA CAKE

SERVES 6–8

PREPARATION
10 minutes

COOKING
50 minutes

WINE

It's always hard to go past a cup of tea or coffee with a cake like this, but a dessert wine would also do the trick.

160 g (5½ oz/1 cup) wholemeal (whole-wheat) flour
1 teaspoon ground cinnamon
1 teaspoon bicarbonate of soda (baking soda)
140 g (5 oz/1 cup) macadamia nuts, roughly chopped
220 g (8 oz/1 cup) raw (demerara) sugar
160 g (5½ oz/1 cup) sultanas (golden raisins)

235 g (8½ oz/1½ cups) finely grated carrot (about 3 medium carrots), firmly packed
2 eggs, lightly beaten
125 ml (4 fl oz/½ cup) macadamia oil

CREAM CHEESE FROSTING
20 g (¾ oz) butter, softened
125 g (4½ oz/½ cup) cream cheese
80 g (2¾ oz/½ cup) icing (confectioners') sugar
1 teaspoon grated orange zest

Preheat the oven to 170°C (340°F).

Grease and line the base of a 20 cm (8 in) round cake tin with baking paper.

Sift the flour, cinnamon and bicarbonate of soda into a bowl. Add the macadamia nuts, sugar, sultanas and carrot and mix well. Add the eggs and oil and stir until all the ingredients are combined.

Pour the batter into the prepared cake tin and bake for 50 minutes. The cake is cooked when a skewer inserted in the centre is removed dry with no clinging batter. However, if it is not cooked after 50 minutes, cover with foil and cook for a further 10–20 minutes. Allow to cool.

For the cream cheese frosting, beat the butter and cream cheese together with a hand-held electric beater until fluffy. Add the icing sugar and beat on a low speed until smooth. Lastly, stir through the orange zest. Spoon the frosting onto the cooled cake, cut the cake into slices and serve.

TOP: Lyndey holding the finished Very berry trifle (recipe page 125).

BOTTOM: Lyndey on a camel safari on Lighthouse Beach, near Port Macquarie, with camel whisperer John Hardy.

Roma (plum) tomatoes

Grape kumatoes

Heirloom beefsteak tomatoes

Truss tomatoes

Kumatoes

Truss cherry tomatoes

Truss baby roma (plum) tomatoes

Green salad tomatoes

Golden grape tomatoes

Carmine tomatoes

TOMATOES

Tomatoes are one of the most versatile fruits, but are usually treated like a vegetable. Finding a naturally ripened tomato is cause for joy, and therefore they are always best in summer. They should be deeply coloured, give a little when squeezed and smell like tomatoes! Store them at room temperature in a single layer. Many are grown hydroponically but, whatever way they are grown, vine-ripened is absolutely the best. Increasingly heirloom varieties are becoming available. In miniature they can be cherry, baby roma (plum), grape, truss and in a variety of colours from yellow to green to red. In the larger sizes there are many of the same varieties but also the almost black kumato and the old-fashioned oxheart.

TOMATO IDEAS

Tomatoes are versatile and can be used in both sweet and savoury dishes. They are essential to Italian cuisine, where they may be eaten raw and drizzled with olive oil, made into soups or sauces, smeared on pizza, diced on bruschetta, semi-dried or sun-dried for antipasto and preserved in tins or jars. In France they are essential to ratatouille, tarts and also make a great tart tatin. In Asia they can be stirred into a curry before serving or made into fiery pastes or chutneys. In Greece tomatoes are stuffed with rice. In the Americas they are used in salsas. Try pressing ripe tomatoes with a plate over a colander for intense tomato consommé, or roasting them to intensify the flavour before puréeing for a soup or sauce. If all else fails, make a Bloody Mary!

For this simple salad I used different tomatoes from Ricardoes Tomatoes &
Strawberries in Port Macquarie including roma (plum), conchita and flavorino
in a variety of colours from green through to rich red. The recipe's success
depends on naturally ripe tomatoes. Heirloom varieties work well, too.

TOMATO SALAD WITH HERB DRESSING

SERVES 4

PREPARATION
10 minutes

1 kg (2 lb 3 oz) assorted tomatoes
½ bunch chives, roughly chopped
½ bunch mint, leaves picked

½ bunch basil, leaves picked
sea salt flakes
1 loaf sourdough, sliced

Slice the tomatoes into large chunks or leave them whole if small and place in a
serving bowl.

   Place the chives, mint and basil in a mortar and sprinkle generously with sea salt flakes.
Using a pestle, pound to grind the herbs and salt into a smooth paste. Spoon over the
tomatoes and serve with the sourdough bread.

WINE

Most likely you will be
eating this side dish
with a main course,
so stick to the wine
which suits that. If,
however, this is the
main event, you can't
go past a semillon or
a chambourcin, the
red grape variety that
flourishes in the Port
Macquarie area.

Although mostly used as a vegetable, tomatoes work really well as a fruit, which is indeed what they are. These flavours make for an unusual and stunning dessert. It's an evolution of a recipe I developed for a previous book, but I used strawberries, which Ricardoes Tomatoes & Strawberries in Port Macquarie grow.

SPICED SWEET TOMATOES

SERVES 4

PREPARATION
5 minutes

COOKING
16 minutes

WINE

Semillon has a natural affinity with tomatoes and, as this is sweet, a botrytised semillon would be perfect.

LYNDEY'S NOTE

If desired, when the tomatoes are cooked, remove them from the saucepan with a slotted spoon, increase the heat and reduce the syrup until thick before drizzling over the tomatoes to serve.

4 ripe but firm tomatoes
1 tablespoon lemon juice
thick Greek-style yoghurt to serve

FILLING
165 g (6 oz) strawberries, washed, hulled and finely diced
6 mint leaves, chopped
1 teaspoon fresh ginger, finely chopped
pinch of freshly ground black pepper
1 teaspoon grated orange zest (see syrup)

SYRUP
190 ml (6½ fl oz/¾ cup) orange juice
145 g (5 oz/⅔ cup) caster (superfine) sugar
zest and juice of 1 orange (less 1 teaspoon zest used in the filling)
zest and juice of 1 lemon
1 teaspoon vanilla bean paste
½ teaspoon ground ginger
2 cloves
2 star anise

To make the syrup, place all the ingredients in a large saucepan or medium frying pan with high sides (big enough to hold the four tomatoes) and boil for 5 minutes.

Meanwhile, cut a slice from the stalk end of each tomato and discard. Scoop out the tomato pulp and discard, leaving the tomato shell. Combine the filling ingredients and stuff each tomato with it.

Place the tomatoes in the saucepan with the syrup and cook over medium–high heat for 10 minutes, basting frequently. When the tomatoes are candied, drizzle them with the lemon juice and cook for a further minute. Remove with a slotted spoon. Serve warm or cold, topped with orange zest from the syrup and yoghurt.

These are inspired by the fried green tomatoes which traditionally feature the 'Southern' American flavours of cayenne pepper, dried thyme and sweet paprika. I've substituted Italian herbs and served them alongside a bright, zingy gremolata made more substantial with the addition of green olives.

FRIED GREEN TOMATOES WITH GREEN OLIVE GREMOLATA

SERVES 8 as a canapé

PREPARATION
15 minutes

COOKING
10 minutes

WINE

These flavours are high acid, naturally paired with sparkling chambourcin but any sparkling wine with low sugar has the added benefit of bubbles, to cleanse the palate of these deep-fried morsels.

LYNDEY'S NOTE

I used sparkling chambourcin because it is a local Port Macquarie wine, but if you don't want to specially open a bottle, simply increase the quantity of sparkling water by 2 tablespoons.

50 g (1¾ oz/⅓ cup) plain (all-purpose) flour
85 g (3 oz/½ cup) polenta
80 ml (2½ fl oz/⅓ cup) sparkling water
2 tablespoons sparkling chambourcin, shiraz or other sparkling red wine
1 egg white
1 teaspoon dried oregano (optional)
1 teaspoon dried basil (optional)
½ teaspoon sweet paprika
½ teaspoon dried red chilli flakes
vegetable oil for deep-frying

500 g (1 lb 2 oz) cherry tomatoes (preferably greenish with a tinge of red)
salt to taste

GREEN OLIVE GREMOLATA
90 g (3 oz/½ cup) green olives, pitted and finely chopped
2 garlic cloves, finely chopped
½ bunch flat-leaf (Italian) parsley, finely chopped
1 teaspoon finely grated lemon zest
salt and freshly ground black pepper to taste

For the green olive gremolata, combine all the ingredients in a small bowl.

Combine the flour, polenta, sparkling water, sparkling wine, egg white, oregano, basil, sweet paprika and chilli flakes in a small bowl and whisk until smooth to make a batter.

Pour the oil into a medium saucepan to a depth of 6 cm (2½ in) and heat over medium heat.

Test the oil by dropping in a small amount of batter — it is ready to cook when the batter turns golden and crisp. Skewer the tomatoes, dip into the batter and, using another skewer, slide into the hot oil. Fry in batches for 2 minutes or until golden and crisp. Drain on paper towel, sprinkle with salt and serve immediately on a platter scattered with the green olive gremolata.

THE
BUSH

Lyndey inspecting the fleece with Craig Starr
at Gold Creek Station outside Canberra.

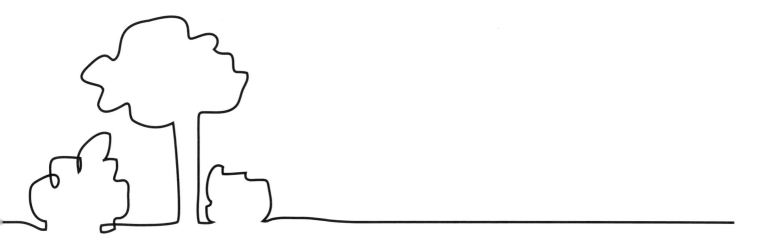

Only 1.8 million Australians of our 23.3 million population live in rural areas. Yet 'the bush' has an important place in the Australian psyche. It has been revered as a source of national ideas by poets such as Henry Lawson and Banjo Paterson, celebrated by the Heidelberg school of artists, including Tom Roberts, Arthur Streeton and Frederick McCubbin, and also by country singers like Slim Dusty and John Williamson. Other writers, poets, artists and songwriters have followed as have movies and it was in the bush that the concept of Australian 'mateship' developed. More importantly, it is in the bush that we feel more connected with Indigenous Australia and are finally embracing some native foods. Yet 'the bush' is a feeling that can mean everything from big country towns and lush pasturelands to the harsh outback or thriving vineyards.

Canberra, the seat of government in Australia, is also sometimes known as the Bush Capital. The name Canberra is thought to mean 'meeting place', derived from the Aboriginal word *kamberra*. Famously chosen because it was between Sydney and Melbourne, the city was designed by architect Walter Burley Griffin.

Floriade is a floral extravaganza held every spring with colourful displays of over a million bulbs and annuals. Lake Burley Griffin is a popular venue for dragon boat racing, a Chinese sport that is more than 2000 years old. I had fun with a female team ranging in ages from 13 to 70 – though with the very early morning start the temperature was below zero! Things warmed up at a working pastoral property at family-run Gold Creek Station. Here visitors can experience sheep mustering, shearing and, for me, tractor driving. To wash it all down, there are 33 cool-climate wineries within 35 minutes of Canberra, with Murrumbateman winemaker Ken Helm staging an annual international Riesling Challenge. Another highlight was visiting the smokehouse, farm shop and café of Poachers Pantry.

Further south on the New South Wales–Victoria border lies the historic town of Albury, nestled on the banks of the mighty Murray River. At the crossroads of regional exploration, it stands as a reminder of the determination and hard work of previous generations who survived flood, drought and the gold rush. The arrival of the first train from Melbourne into Albury in 1873 largely spelt the end of the paddlesteam era for the Murray River and changed the face of both Albury and travel in regional towns forever. The Albury railway station, opened in 1881, has the longest railway platform in the southern hemisphere and was an important transfer point between Sydney and Melbourne.

The Hume Murray Farmers Markets in Albury are a showcase for regional produce, including cheese, award-winning ice cream, smallgoods, locally grown meats, wines, plants and herbs – the perfect ingredients to cook in the communal wood-fired oven in Hovell Tree Park, regularly fired up by an expert for all to enjoy. I was there on Grandparents Day and the park was alive with people of all ages, queueing up to put their pizzas and other creations in the oven. I was also there for the Albury Races where I joined the locals who had dusted off their fascinators and suits for a flutter on the horses.

The region abounds with native produce. The Murray Bank Yabby Farm, west of Albury, is a little haven where visitors can stay and play. I loved catching my own yabbies. The farm also makes and sells marmalade, to honour their late grandson Stewart and raises money for a charity in his memory, Stewart's Way, which helps educate Nepalese children.

Nearby, the Wonga Wetlands have a special place in the hearts of the Wiradjuri people, the traditional landowners of the area. The wetlands are rich with yabbies, Murray cod, yellow belly, kangaroos, emus and an abundance of plant life, including wattleseed and medicinal plants. This was one of the most moving experiences for me. I was blown away when local woman Leonie McIntosh, who has learned the ways of the bush from her elders, handed me a stone tool, like a mortar and pestle. As I felt it, I imagined all the hands which must have used it – especially when she told me it was at the very least 2000 years old. When I asked her the best advice her revered grandmother had given her she said, 'Education. Education is the key to our survival. Our cultural survival as well as our people's survival. Without education we can't share our culture, we can't get and give things a go.'

When visiting the Helm winery, one of the first commercial wineries in the Canberra district, my old friend Ken Helm took me fly fishing for rainbow trout using a bogong moth fly. Believe me, it's harder than it looks, but fortunately he already had some rainbow trout and, more importantly, some riesling! So I devised this simple but beautiful recipe.

RAINBOW TROUT WITH PRESERVED LEMON AND HERB DRESSING

SERVES 2

PREPARATION
10 minutes

COOKING
5–10 minutes

WINE

The flavours here are light and delicate and the citrus flavours in the dressing match superbly with the lemony notes in a riesling.

LYNDEY'S NOTE

Sprinkling the skin side of the trout with flour prior to cooking is a great way to ensure crisp skin. Covering with a lid avoids having to turn the fish, as it steams through.

2 small zucchini (courgettes), sliced
　　lengthways into 1 cm (½ in) ribbons
1 bunch asparagus, woody ends removed
2 x 200 g (7 oz) rainbow trout fillets,
　　skin on
1 tablespoon plain (all-purpose) flour
salt and freshly ground black pepper
　　to taste
1 tablespoon extra-virgin olive oil
20 g (¾ oz) butter

**PRESERVED LEMON AND
HERB DRESSING**
2 tablespoons tarragon leaves, shredded
60 ml (2 fl oz/¼ cup) extra-virgin olive oil
juice of ½ lemon
¼ preserved lemon, flesh discarded and
　　rind finely chopped
salt and freshly ground black pepper
　　to taste

For the preserved lemon and herb dressing, put all the ingredients in a small bowl and whisk well to combine. Season to taste with salt and pepper.

Heat a cast-iron chargrill pan over medium heat. Cook the zucchini and asparagus (in batches if necessary), brushing frequently with the preserved lemon and herb dressing until charred and tender. Reserve the remaining dressing.

Meanwhile, coat the trout, skin side only, with flour seasoned with salt and pepper. Heat the oil and butter in a large frying pan with a lid over medium heat, add the trout, skin side down, and cook for a couple of minutes or until beginning to brown. Cover with the lid and cook for another couple of minutes, or until the fish is opaque and cooked through.

Serve the trout on a bed of the vegetables, drizzled with the reserved dressing.

I was delighted to visit Susan Bruce at Poachers Pantry just outside Canberra, whose smoked food products I have enjoyed for 21 years, as well as their Wily Trout wines. Paul D'Monte, head chef at their Smokehouse Café shared this recipe. As he says, this is 'a great winter dish to share with friends and family. This recipe is for two people but can be easily adapted to cater for larger groups.'

DUCK LEG WITH CHERRIES, SMOKED DUCK BREAST, WITLOF AND ROSÉ JUS

SERVES 2

PREPARATION
5 minutes

COOKING
1 hour 15 minutes

WINE
Duck and pinot noir are the eighth wonder of the world when consumed together!

20 g (¾ oz) butter
2 witlof (Belgian endives/chicory)
500 ml (17 fl oz/2 cups) veal or beef stock
salt
2 tablespoons sugar
1 tablespoon extra-virgin olive oil
2 duck leg quarters (thigh and leg)
1 thyme sprig
125 ml (4 fl oz/½ cup) rosé
1½ tablespoons red wine vinegar

zest and juice of 1 orange
2 garlic cloves, finely chopped
100 g (3½ oz) cherries or sour cherries, pitted
1 small smoked duck breast (about 180 g/ 6½ oz), ideally from Poachers Pantry

Heat the butter in a medium frying pan over medium–high heat. Slice the witlof in half lengthways and place, cut side down, in the pan. Add 250 ml (8½ fl oz/1 cup) of the stock, salt and 1 tablespoon of the sugar. Simmer for 10 minutes or until soft. Drain and set aside.

Add the oil to the pan. Season the duck legs with salt and brown them very well all over. Add the thyme, remaining stock and rosé to cover, and simmer over low heat for 1 hour at least or until tender, but do not boil. When tender, remove the duck legs from the stock and set aside to rest in a warm place, covered loosely with foil.

Increase the heat under the pan to high, add the vinegar, remaining sugar, orange zest and juice, garlic and cherries. Reduce by two-thirds or until thickened and sauce-like.

Meanwhile score the fat of the smoked duck breast, then place in a small clean frying pan, skin side down, over medium heat to crisp and warm through. Remove from the pan and slice thinly. Add the witlof to the pan to reheat and caramelise.

Serve the duck leg quarters with the duck breast, witlof and sauce.

A traditional Australian Sunday roast in finger food form. This was one of a trio of recipes I cooked outside historic Albury railway station, taking my inspiration from foods popular during the times of grand train travel.

MUSTARD PIKELETS WITH MINTED LAMB

MAKES 30

PREPARATION
10 minutes

COOKING
20 minutes

WINE
The soft, gentle flavours of a merlot work well here.

2 tablespoons extra-virgin olive oil
200 g (7 oz) lamb tenderloins (fillets)
salt and freshly ground black pepper
2 tablespoons white wine vinegar
2 teaspoons caster (superfine) sugar
¼ cup shredded mint leaves

MUSTARD PIKELETS
160 g (5½ oz/1 cup) wholemeal (whole-wheat) self-raising flour
1 egg
125 ml (4 fl oz/½ cup) milk
2 tablespoons extra-virgin olive oil
2 tablespoons wholegrain mustard
butter to cook

To make the mustard pikelets, place the flour in a large bowl, make a well in the centre and add the egg, milk, oil and mustard. Whisk until smooth.

Melt a teaspoon of butter in a large non-stick frying pan. Swirl to coat the base, then place heaped teaspoons of the pikelet mixture in the foaming butter. Cook until set around the edges, flip over and cook for another minute or until golden and cooked through. Drain on paper towel and repeat with the remaining mixture, cleaning the pan after each batch with paper towel and adding another teaspoon of butter.

Heat 1 tablespoon of the olive oil in the pan over medium heat. Season the lamb with salt and pepper and cook for 3 minutes before turning and cooking for an additional minute for medium, or longer if desired. Remove from the pan, cover with foil and set aside to rest for 5 minutes before slicing into very thin slices.

Whisk the white wine vinegar and caster sugar with the remaining tablespoon of oil in a medium bowl. Add the mint and sliced lamb and season to taste with salt and pepper.

Serve the pikelets topped with the dressed slices of lamb and the mint leaves.

146

There is nothing more Australian than roast lamb, but we are also fast adopters of new flavours. Serve this with Pumpkin purée (page 158) and Roasted finger eggplant with spiced tahini drizzle (page 160) and/or a crisp salad.

LAMB SHOULDER WITH MIDDLE EASTERN SPICES

SERVES 4

PREPARATION
10 minutes

COOKING 2 hours
10 minutes,
plus resting

WINE

The tartness from the pomegranate cuts through the richness of the lamb, so this dish is best with a shiraz – or try a spicy merlot.

LYNDEY'S NOTE

Pomegranate molasses is a thick reduction of pomegranate juice, made by boiling the liquid to a syrup. The flavour is sweetly tart and brings astringency and sourness to dishes in a similar way to lemon juice or tamarind. Substitute caramelised balsamic with a squeeze of lemon juice.

1 lamb shoulder on the bone, approximately 2 kg (4 lb 6 oz)
2 teaspoons sea salt
2 teaspoons ground cumin
2 teaspoons sweet paprika
½ teaspoon cayenne pepper
1 tablespoon extra-virgin olive oil
2 brown onions
2 garlic bulbs, halved crossways
1 tablespoon pomegranate molasses

Remove the lamb from the refrigerator at least 30 minutes prior to cooking. Preheat the oven to 200°C (400°F).

Combine the salt, cumin, paprika and cayenne pepper and rub over both sides of the lamb.

Heat a large frying pan over high heat. Add the oil and brown the lamb, skin side down, for 5 minutes or until golden. Turn and cook for a further 5 minutes.

Peel the onions and slice into 5 mm (¼ in) rounds, being careful not to separate the slices into rings. Place the rounds in the base of a large baking dish, top with the lamb, skin side up, and put the garlic beside it. Drizzle the pomegranate molasses over the lamb. Pour 250 ml (8½ fl oz/1 cup) water around the lamb. Cover with foil and place in the oven for 1 hour.

Uncover, reduce the heat to 180°C (350°F) and roast for an additional hour or until the meat is very tender. Remove from the oven and rest, covered with foil, for 15 minutes.

Meanwhile, remove any excess fat from the juices and onions in the baking dish (either with a fat/lean (gravy separator) pitcher or by scooping it off the top). Place the baking dish over medium heat and boil to reduce a little.

Carve the lamb and serve each person with a half bulb of garlic so they can scoop out its tender flesh. Serve with the onion sauce.

I first tried licorice sauce when I was filming the TV show Lyndey Milan's Taste of Ireland. I loved its unique flavour, so I developed my own sauce recipe and found it paired really well with kangaroo. The parsnip colcannon, usually made with potato, is in honour of the many Irish who settled in Australia.

SEARED KANGAROO LOIN WITH LICORICE SAUCE AND PARSNIP COLCANNON

SERVES 4

PREPARATION
20 minutes

COOKING
25 minutes

1 tablespoon extra-virgin olive oil
750 g (1 lb 11 oz) kangaroo loin fillets
salt and freshly ground black pepper
500 ml (17 fl oz/2 cups) beef or veal stock
125 ml (4 fl oz/½ cup) dry sherry
1½ tablespoons redcurrant jelly
1½ tablespoons licorice root, chopped
1 tablespoon apple cider vinegar
wilted spinach to serve (optional)

PARSNIP COLCANNON
3 parsnips (about 600 g/1 lb 5 oz in total), peeled and cut into 5 cm (2 in) pieces
40 g (1½ oz) butter
190 g (6½ oz/2½ cups) finely shredded cavolo nero (Tuscan cabbage) or savoy cabbage
1 brown onion, thinly sliced
1 leek, thinly sliced
60 ml (2 fl oz/¼ cup) milk
salt and freshly ground black pepper

For the parsnip colcannon, place the parsnips in a large saucepan, cover with cold water and bring to the boil. Simmer for 25 minutes, or until tender.

Meanwhile, melt 20 g (¾ oz) of the butter in a medium frying pan and add the cabbage, onion and leek. Cook over medium heat, stirring frequently, for 6 minutes or until tender. Drain the parsnips and leave them to steam for a few minutes before pushing them through a potato ricer, mouli grater or sieve back into the saucepan.

Heat the milk and the remaining butter in a small saucepan or in the microwave. Pour the milk mixture over the parsnips and beat well. Fold through the cabbage mixture and season to taste with salt and pepper. Keep warm until needed.

Preheat the oven to 200°C (400°F).

WINE

Kangaroo is a gamey meat and the licorice sauce is a little aniseed-like, so go for a shiraz or grenache.

Heat a large frying pan over high heat and add the olive oil. If the kangaroo loins are too long for the diameter of your pan, cut them in half crossways. Season the kangaroo with salt and pepper and brown quickly on all sides for 3 minutes. Remove the kangaroo to a baking tray and roast in the oven for 6 minutes for rare. (Alternatively cook in a covered pan, turning once until cooked as desired.) Cover loosely with foil and rest for 5–10 minutes.

Meanwhile return the kangaroo frying pan to the heat and add the stock, sherry, redcurrant jelly and licorice root. Bring to the boil, stirring to dissolve the redcurrant jelly and disgorge any sediment. Add any kangaroo juices. Boil over medium–high heat until thickened and reduced by approximately half. Strain into a small saucepan, discarding the licorice root. Add the apple cider vinegar to taste and season with salt and pepper. Keep warm until needed.

To serve, place a spoonful of the warm parsnip colcannon on each plate. Top with thick slices of kangaroo and drizzle with licorice sauce. Serve with wilted spinach, if desired.

Crumbing meat is a time-honoured tradition. While crumbed lamb cutlets, mash and peas have a fond place in most Australians' hearts, veal makes a lighter alternative, especially with panko crumbs. For Paris mash, use cream rather than milk in the mashed potato recipe, double the quantity of butter and sieve the mash at least once, using a fork, potato ricer or drum sieve, for a silky texture.

VEAL SCHNITZEL WITH MASHED POTATO AND SMASHED PEAS

SERVES 4

PREPARATION
15 minutes

COOKING
40 minutes

WINE

A white wine with some texture is called for, like a chardonnay, marsanne or roussanne. Or go for a softer style of red, such as an Italian varietal like barbera or sangiovese.

2 garlic cloves, finely chopped
1 egg, beaten
60 g (2 oz/1 cup) panko crumbs
2 tablespoons flat-leaf (Italian) parsley, finely chopped
zest of 1 small lemon plus the cheeks of 2 lemons
sea salt and freshly ground black pepper
2 tablespoons plain (all-purpose) flour
4 x 180 g (6½ oz) veal schnitzels
80 ml (2½ fl oz/⅓ cup) extra-virgin olive oil for shallow-frying

MASHED POTATO
650 g (1 lb 7 oz) evenly sized floury potatoes, such as pontiac, sebago or king edward, washed
1 teaspoon salt
freshly ground black pepper
85 g (3 oz) butter, diced, at room temperature
125 ml (4 fl oz/½ cup) milk, warmed

SMASHED PEAS
1 mint sprig
pinch of sugar
400 g (14 oz/3⅓ cups) frozen peas

For the mashed potatoes, place the potatoes in a large saucepan, cover with cold water and add the salt. Bring to the boil over high heat. Reduce the heat to medium and simmer, uncovered, for 30 minutes or until very soft.

Meanwhile, for the smashed peas, bring a large saucepan of salted water to the boil. Add the mint, sugar and peas and boil for 4 minutes or until tender. Drain, reserving 2 tablespoons of the cooking water. Transfer the peas and reserved cooking water to a large bowl and mash with a fork or potato masher. The idea is to keep some texture. Set aside and keep warm.

For the veal, combine the garlic and egg in a medium bowl. Combine the panko crumbs, parsley, lemon zest, sea salt and pepper on a flat plate. Place the flour on another flat plate and season with salt and pepper. Dip the schnitzels in the seasoned flour and shake off the excess. Dip in the egg, and then in the breadcrumb mixture, pressing to coat.

»»»

LYNDEY'S NOTE

Panko are Japanese breadcrumbs. They are made from crustless bread, making them light and flaky. They also absorb less oil and can be found in the Asian section of all good supermarkets.

Drain the potatoes and return them to the saucepan. Shake the pan over low heat for 15–30 seconds to remove the remaining moisture. Remove the saucepan from the heat, cover with a clean tea towel (dish towel) and leave for 5 minutes. Peel the skins. If not dry and flaky, return the potatoes to the dry saucepan and shake over low heat for another 15–30 seconds.

Mash the potatoes with a potato ricer, mouli grater or hand masher, with the diced butter, salt and pepper, until smooth. Add half the warm milk to the pan, beat in with a fork, metal whisk or wooden spoon, then slowly add the remaining milk and beat again until well incorporated. Set aside and keep warm.

Heat half the olive oil in a large non-stick frying pan over high heat. Fry the veal in two batches for 1–2 minutes on each side, until just cooked and golden. Drain on paper towel. In between each batch wipe down the pan to remove any burning crumbs and heat the remaining oil. Serve immediately with the mashed potato, smashed peas and lemon cheeks.

This recipe couldn't be further from the gloopy bright orange sweet and sour pork of old. Luscious pork belly is flavoured with traditional Cantonese Chinese flavours, roasted until the crackling is crisp and livened up with a pineapple pickle bursting with freshness, the perfect foil to the richness of the pork belly. Serve with Wok-tossed greens (page 159).

PEKING PORK BELLY WITH PINEAPPLE PICKLE

SERVES 4–6

PREPARATION
20 minutes, plus optional 2 hours refrigeration

COOKING 1½ hours

WINE

A pinot noir, wonderful with the Chinese flavours, can also handle the acid in the pickle. White wine drinkers may prefer verdelho.

1.5 kg (3 lb 5 oz) boneless pork belly, ideally of even thickness
1 teaspoon salt
coriander (cilantro) sprigs to serve

PINEAPPLE PICKLE
80 ml (2½ fl oz/⅓ cup) Chinese black vinegar
2–4 teaspoons caster (superfine) sugar (depending on sweetness of pineapple)
1 large red chilli, thinly sliced
½ pineapple, peeled, cored and thinly sliced lengthways

1 small cucumber, seeded and cut into long matchsticks
1 large carrot, peeled and cut into long ribbons

SAUCE
1 tablespoon Chinese five-spice
2 teaspoons sea salt flakes
60 ml (2 fl oz/¼ cup) dark soy sauce
2 tablespoons hoisin sauce
55 g (2 oz/¼ cup) firmly packed brown sugar
3 garlic cloves, finely chopped
3 cm (1¼ in) piece ginger, finely chopped

Using a very sharp knife, score the pork belly rind by making diagonal cuts 1 cm (½ in) apart across the whole surface to create a diamond pattern. Place in a colander or on a wire rack in the sink and pour over a kettle full of boiling water to help the rind separate. If necessary, score more lines. Dry well with paper towel and place, uncovered, in the refrigerator for 2 hours or even overnight. Remove from the refrigerator 30 minutes prior to cooking and rub the rind with salt.

Preheat the oven to 220°C (430°F). Wipe the pork well with paper towel to remove any excess moisture and place, rind side up, in a baking dish not much bigger than the pork and roast for 30 minutes.

For the sauce, combine the Chinese five-spice and salt in a small frying pan and toss over high heat for 2 minutes or until fragrant. Combine the salt mixture with the remaining ingredients in a pitcher.

»»»

Use a vegetable peeler to slice the vegetables for the pickle. Disposable aluminium trays 32 cm x 26 cm (12¾ in x 10¼ in) are a perfect size for 1.5 kg (3 lb 5 oz) pork belly and save on washing up!

Remove the pork from the oven and reduce the heat to 180°C (350°F). Lift the pork from the baking dish, pour the sauce into the baking dish and place the pork on top, ensuring no sauce gets on the rind. Return to the oven and roast for an additional hour or until the rind is crisp and translucent and the meat juices run clear. If the juices are clear and the rind is not crisp enough, remove the rind and put it under a grill (broiler) for 5 minutes or until the rind blisters. Remove to a wire rack to rest.

Meanwhile prepare the pineapple pickle by combining the Chinese black vinegar with the caster sugar and chilli in a small saucepan over low heat. Stir until the sugar dissolves, increase the heat, bring to the boil and simmer for 2 minutes. Pour over the pineapple, cucumber and carrot and set aside until serving.

To serve, cut the pork into thin slices and serve with the pineapple pickle topped with the coriander sprigs.

Pumpkin (winter squash) is one of Australia's favourite vegetables, especially baked. It can also be barbecued, steamed or mashed. It's much easier to purée than potatoes because you can use a food processor or hand-held blender.

PUMPKIN PURÉE

SERVES 4 as a side

PREPARATION
5 minutes

COOKING
10 minutes

300 g (10½ oz) pumpkin (winter squash), peeled and cut into wedges
20 g (¾ oz) butter

salt and freshly ground black pepper to taste

Steam or microwave the pumpkin until tender. Do not boil, as it will absorb too much water. Drain well.

Process or blend the pumpkin with the butter until smooth. Season to taste with salt and pepper. Serve.

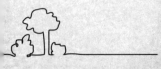

Serve this with anything with Asian flavours, such as the Peking pork belly with pineapple pickle (page 155).

WOK-TOSSED GREENS

SERVES 4 as a side

PREPARATION 10 minutes

COOKING 5 minutes

LYNDEY'S NOTE

If I'm not serving these greens with a strongly flavoured recipe, I like to add 2 finely chopped garlic cloves and a 3 cm (1¼ in) piece fresh ginger, finely chopped, with the asparagus and sugar snap peas. Tamari is (usually) a wheat-free soy sauce, although regular soy sauce can be substituted.

1 bunch baby bok choy (pak choy) (about 400 g/14 oz)
1 tablespoon extra-virgin olive oil
1 bunch asparagus, sliced into 5 cm (2 in) lengths diagonally

150 g (5½ oz) sugar snap peas
1 teaspoon sesame oil
1 tablespoon tamari
salt and freshly ground black pepper to taste

Prepare the bok choy by slicing lengthways into quarters. Soak in cold water to remove any grit. Drain well and dry with paper towel before using.

Heat a wok over high heat. Add the olive oil, asparagus and sugar snap peas and toss for 1 minute. Add the bok choy, sesame oil and tamari and continue to toss for another minute or until the vegetables are just tender. Season to taste with salt and pepper and serve immediately.

These thin eggplants (aubergines) are sometimes also known as Japanese or Lebanese eggplants.

ROASTED FINGER EGGPLANT WITH SPICED TAHINI DRIZZLE

SERVES 4 as a side dish

PREPARATION
10 minutes

COOKING
15 minutes

8 baby eggplants (aubergines) (about 480 g/1 lb 1 oz in total)
2 tablespoons extra-virgin olive oil
salt and freshly ground black pepper to taste
2 tablespoons tahini
1 tablespoon thick Greek-style yoghurt

1 tablespoon lemon juice
1 garlic clove, finely chopped
½ teaspoon ground cumin
¼ teaspoon dried red chilli flakes
2 tablespoons flat-leaf (Italian) parsley, roughly chopped, to serve
2 tablespoons toasted pine nuts to serve

Preheat the oven to 200°C (400°F) and line a baking tray with baking paper.

Prepare the eggplants by slicing them in half lengthways. Place them, cut side up, on the prepared baking tray, drizzle with the oil and season with salt and pepper to taste. Roast for 15 minutes or until golden and cooked through.

Meanwhile, combine the tahini, yoghurt, lemon juice, garlic, cumin and chilli. Mix well and season to taste with salt and pepper. If the mixture is too thick to drizzle, add 1 tablespoon water and mix well until smooth.

Serve the eggplant drizzled with the tahini mixture and scattered with the flat-leaf parsley and pine nuts.

Floriade, the annual floral spectacular in Canberra, was the perfect location for chef Claude Fremy to cook this for me. He garnished it with flowers and spun sugar. I thought I'd keep it simple, but you can use any edible flowers you have to hand.

LAVENDER CRÈME BRÛLÉE

SERVES 6

PREPARATION
10 minutes

COOKING 1 hour
5 minutes, plus
chilling time

WINE

Desserts are always best matched with a dessert wine. Traditionally these were botrytised semillons but increasingly other white varietals are used, too.

LYNDEY'S NOTE

Lavender syrup is made by bringing 300 g (10½ oz) sugar and 300 ml (10 fl oz) water to the boil, simmering for 5 minutes then infusing with up to 1 cup of washed lavender. Strain before use.

500 ml (17 fl oz/2 cups) pouring (single/light) cream
3 tablespoons dried lavender leaves
2 vanilla beans
6 large egg yolks
180 g (6½ oz) caster (superfine) sugar

CARAMEL
110 g (4 oz/½ cup) sugar
80 ml (2½ fl oz/⅓ cup) water

FLOWER GARNISH
1 tablespoon stevia (optional), finely chopped
1 tablespoon peppermint leaves, finely chopped
1 cup edible flowers, such as pansies, borage, chamomile and cornflowers
1–2 tablespoons lavender syrup (see Lyndey's note)
½–1 teaspoon lemon juice

Preheat the oven to 120°C (250°F).

Place six shallow (2.5 cm/1 in high and 10 cm/4 in diameter) crème brûlée dishes or ramekins on a baking tray.

Place the cream and lavender in a medium saucepan. Slit the vanilla beans lengthways and scrape out the seeds. Add both to the saucepan and bring to the boil over medium heat. Remove from the heat, cover and leave to infuse.

Whisk the egg yolks and 3 tablespoons of the caster sugar together until well blended and, while still whisking, strain and drizzle in a quarter of the infused cream (to temper the yolks, to prevent the mixture from curdling). Pour in the rest of the liquid, mix to combine and pour it into the baking dishes.

Bake the crème brûlées for 40–60 minutes, or until set but still slightly wobbly in the centre. Let the crème brûlées cool until they reach room temperature. Cover each with plastic wrap and refrigerate for at least 3 hours.

For the caramel, place the sugar and water in a medium saucepan over medium heat and stir only until the sugar dissolves. Cook for a few minutes until the caramel starts to turn golden. Once caramelised, drizzle onto a sheet of baking paper and make decorative shapes to place on top of the crème brûlées.

Combine the flower garnish ingredients gently.

To serve, sprinkle each crème brûlée evenly with 1 tablespoon of the caster sugar, then brown the sugar with a blowtorch until it bubbles and colours. Top with the caramel decorations and flower garnish.

The grandeur and leisurely pace of train travel is reflected in Albury's beautiful railway station so, as a nod to times past, I cooked up my own high tea with a twist. These meringues are a modern take on an Australian classic — the pavlova with cream and passionfruit. Made as miniatures, they are ideal for afternoon tea or to finish a cocktail party.

BROWN SUGAR MERINGUES WITH PASSIONFRUIT CURD

MAKES 50

PREPARATION
15 minutes

COOKING
50 minutes

3 eggs, separated
80 g (2¾ oz/⅓ cup) caster (superfine) sugar
80 g (2¾ oz/⅓ cup) brown sugar
1 tablespoon cornflour (cornstarch)
1 teaspoon vanilla bean paste
lightly whipped cream to serve

PASSIONFRUIT CURD
60 g (2 oz/¼ cup) passionfruit pulp
40 g (1½ oz) butter
55 g (2 oz/¼ cup) caster (superfine) sugar
3 egg yolks (left over from the meringue mixture)

WINE

If not a perfectly brewed cup of tea or coffee, then a dessert wine, like a botrytised semillon, will match the sweet lemony flavours.

LYNDEY'S NOTE

To test to see if the sugar has dissolved in the meringue, rub a small amount of mixture between your fingers; if gritty, keep beating until it feels smooth.

Preheat the oven to 160°C (320°F) and line two baking trays with baking paper.

Using an electric mixer, beat the egg whites until they form stiff peaks. Add the caster sugar then the brown sugar, gradually, and continue to beat until the mixture is glossy and the sugar dissolves. Add the cornflour and vanilla and mix until just combined.

Spoon or pipe the meringue onto the prepared trays. With the back of a wet teaspoon, carefully make an indent in each meringue that will hold the cream and curd. Bake for 50 minutes or until dry. Place the trays on wire racks and leave to cool. Carefully peel the meringues off the baking paper.

While the meringues are baking, make the passionfruit curd. Strain the passionfruit pulp but return a few seeds to it and put it with the remaining ingredients in a heatproof bowl over simmering water. Whisk for 10 minutes or until thickened. Set aside to cool completely, stirring occasionally to prevent a skin from forming.

To serve, top the meringues with a spoon of the lightly whipped cream and a dollop of the passionfruit curd.

There was a grand dining room in Albury railway station where passengers could enjoy silver service hospitality and high tea. These chocolate morsels use a delicious combination of rose and raspberry in the filling to make a modern and elegant sweet treat for a high tea, morning tea or even a cocktail party.

CHOCOLATE SPONGE KISSES WITH ROSE AND RASPBERRY CREAM

MAKES 35 kisses

PREPARATION
20 minutes

COOKING
12 minutes

TO DRINK
Coffee is a great companion, otherwise try a sparkling shiraz!

LYNDEY'S NOTE
If using frozen raspberries, thaw them out and make sure they are well drained.

125 g (4½ oz) butter, softened
160 g (5½ oz/1 cup) lightly packed brown sugar
1 teaspoon natural vanilla extract
1 egg
70 g (2½ oz/²⁄₃ cup) unsweetened (Dutch) cocoa powder
1 teaspoon bicarbonate of soda (baking soda)
¼ teaspoon salt
225 g (8 oz/1½ cups) plain (all-purpose) flour
170 ml (5½ fl oz/²⁄₃ cup) buttermilk

ROSE AND RASPBERRY FILLING
250 g (9 oz/1 cup) cream cheese, softened
80 g (2¾ oz/½ cup) icing (confectioners') sugar, sifted
1½ teaspoons rosewater
250g (9 oz) raspberries, fresh or frozen (see Lyndey's note)

Preheat the oven to 200°C (400°F) and line two baking trays with baking paper.

Using an electric mixer, beat the butter, brown sugar and vanilla in a large bowl until pale and creamy. Add the egg and beat until combined. Sift the cocoa, bicarbonate of soda and salt into the batter and mix to combine. Fold in half the flour and half the buttermilk and repeat; mixing until well combined. The mixture will be quite thick.

Use a piping bag to pipe 1 teaspoon of mixture at a time onto the prepared trays. Space slightly apart to allow room to spread during cooking. Bake for 12 minutes or until just firm. Place on wire racks to cool completely.

Meanwhile, make the rose and raspberry filling. Using an electric mixer, beat the cream cheese, icing sugar and rosewater until smooth. Add ¼ cup of the raspberries and continue to beat until well incorporated. The mixture will turn a glorious shade of pink.

To serve, spread ½ teaspoon of the filling mixture onto the flat side of each cookie. Top half the cookies with the whole raspberries, placing them around the edge. Sandwich with the remaining cookies, pressing down gently.

Finger limes

Dried bush tomatoes

Warrigal greens

Ground strawberry gum

Pepperberries

Roasted whole wattleseeds

Mountain pepperleaf

Roasted ground wattleseeds

Macadamia nuts

Ground lemon myrtle

Lemon myrtle

NATIVE BUSH FLAVOURS

Australia is a country that had a food culture long before the arrival of white people. I have long been a fan of Indigenous herbs, spices and animals. These ingredients grow naturally in Australia with no need for irrigation but many are now cultivated, giving back to the Indigenous communities involved.

NATIVE BUSH FLAVOUR IDEAS

Warrigal greens, lemon myrtle and finger limes can be bought fresh. Warrigal greens should always be blanched, even if using for salad, to remove the oxalic acid. Then they can be used in the same way as English spinach, silverbeet (Swiss chard) or kale. Lemon myrtle is a sub-tropical flowering plant. The leaves can be dried and ground and used effectively with fish, infused in oils, made into tea and are glorious in sweet treats like cheesecake, ice cream, sorbet and shortbread. (It doesn't curdle like fresh lemon juice does.) Finger limes, also known as 'lime caviar', are filled with seeds that pop with lime flavour. Ranging in colour from pink to green, they are perfect as a garnish on any seafood or used in drinks. Dried spices include bush tomato and akudjura, native berries with a caramel yet tangy flavour. Available whole or ground, they can be used in casseroles or to flavour proteins, especially when blended with coriander and wattleseed. Only some wattles are edible and they can be infused to flavour ice cream and desserts or on barbecued meats or seafood. Both the berries and leaves are used from native pepperberry. Much hotter than conventional pepper it has a strong bite, so use it in small quantities. Strawberry gum has an extraordinary berry aroma and can be used to enhance fruit and berry flavours. Macadamia nuts are indigenous to Australia and are exported around the world.

I caught yabbies myself at Murray Bank Yabby Farm near Albury and took inspiration from local Wiradjuri woman Leonie McIntosh to incorporate Indigenous ingredients into this stunning dish.

YABBIES WITH LEMON MYRTLE BUTTER AND MACADAMIA WARRIGAL GREENS

SERVES 4

PREPARATION
15 minutes

COOKING
10 minutes

WINE
The lemony flavours are well suited to a semillon, and the butter dictates an older one with toasty aged flavours.

LYNDEY'S NOTE
Warrigal greens are also known as warrigal spinach, New Zealand spinach or Botany Bay greens. They should always be blanched, even if using for salad, to remove the oxalic acid. You could substitute silverbeet (Swiss chard), English spinach or kale.

16 yabbies
1 tablespoon salt
1 small white onion, roughly chopped
250 ml (8½ fl oz/1 cup) white wine
1 tablespoon native pepperberries
2 tablespoons lemon myrtle leaves
1 flat-leaf (Italian) parsley sprig

LEMON MYRTLE BUTTER
125 ml (4 fl oz/½ cup) white wine
juice of ½ lemon
1 teaspoon ground lemon myrtle

2.5 cm (1 in) piece fresh ginger, peeled and finely chopped
125 g (4½ oz) cold butter, diced

WARRIGAL GREENS
1–2 tablespoons macadamia oil or extra-virgin olive oil
250 g (9 oz) warrigal greens, leaves picked
60 ml (2 fl oz/¼ cup) water (optional)
2 garlic cloves, finely chopped
35 g (1¼ oz/¼ cup) macadamia nuts, lightly toasted and roughly chopped

Place the yabbies in the freezer for 15 minutes to put them to sleep. Meanwhile, place 2 litres (68 fl oz/8 cups) water, the salt, onion, wine, pepperberries, lemon myrtle leaves and parsley in a large stockpot, bring to the boil then reduce the heat to a simmer. Add the yabbies to the pot and poach for 10 minutes or until red in colour and the tails spring back when pressed. Drain and refresh under cold water.

To peel the yabbies, twist off the heads. Using scissors, cut down the side of the shell and peel off; discard. Remove the intestinal tract.

For the lemon myrtle butter, place the wine, lemon juice, lemon myrtle and ginger in a medium saucepan over high heat. Bring to the boil and reduce the liquid by half. Strain and return to the heat then whisk in the butter until all the ingredients emulsify. Remove from the heat.

For the greens, heat 1 tablespoon of the macadamia oil in a large frying pan over medium heat. Add the warrigal greens and cook for 2 minutes or until slightly wilted and bright green in colour. Add the water, if necessary, to help the wilting process. Once wilted, add the garlic and macadamia nuts.

Add the yabby flesh to the same pan as the warrigal greens (with an extra tablespoon of oil, if desired) and flash-fry to brown slightly and heat through.

To serve, divide the warrigal greens among serving plates. Top with four yabbies and spoon over the lemon myrtle butter.

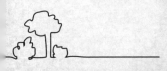

Larb or larp is a popular north-eastern Thai dish and is also the national dish of Laos. Essentially it is a sour and spicy meat, fish or vegetarian salad, fragrant with fresh herbs and spices. There are other regional variations in Thailand and the meat or fish can be cooked whole and shredded or minced (ground) and then cooked with the flavourings. As a fan of Australian native spices, I am using those instead.

BARRAMUNDI 'LARB' WITH NATIVE AUSTRALIAN FLAVOURS

SERVES 4 as an appetiser

PREPARATION
15 minutes

COOKING
15 minutes

WINE

The lemony, herbaceous flavours here are well suited to a riesling or semillon.

LYNDEY'S NOTE

This also makes a lovely canapé in witlof leaves. This amount makes around 24.

50 g (1¾ oz) bean-thread (cellophane) noodles
¾ teaspoon ground lemon myrtle
1 teaspoon ground native pepperberry
salt
2 x 200 g (7 oz) barramundi fillets, skin on
1 tablespoon extra-virgin olive oil
2 garlic cloves, finely chopped

3 cm (1¼ in) piece fresh ginger, finely chopped
80 ml (2½ fl oz/⅓ cup) lime juice and the zest of 1 lime or 2–3 native finger limes
½ cup native mint or mint leaves, roughly chopped, plus a few extra sprigs
1 small red onion, finely chopped
2 witlof (Belgian endives/chicory) or baby gem lettuces, leaves separated

Place the noodles in a large heatproof bowl. Pour over boiling water to cover. Set aside for 5 minutes or until the noodles are tender. Drain well, cut into shorter pieces, cover and set aside.

Combine the lemon myrtle, pepperberry and a good grinding of salt. Dust this mixture on both sides of the barramundi.

Heat the oil in a large frying pan over medium–high heat. Add the barramundi, skin side down, and cook for 4 minutes, then reduce the heat to medium and cook for 2 more minutes or until crusted. Turn over and cook on the other side until cooked through, approximately 4 minutes more. After 2 minutes add the garlic and ginger to the pan, stirring often.

Remove then slide off the crisp skin and reserve. Place the fish flesh in a shallow bowl and, using two forks, flake the fish, mixing through the garlic and ginger. Season with salt, lime juice and zest or fruit from the finger limes, the mint and onion and mix well. Toss through the bean-thread noodles and taste for seasoning. Cut the crisp barramundi skin into thin shards.

To serve, divide the witlof or lettuce leaves among four plates, top with the barramundi mixture, a few sprigs of mint, extra finger lime pearls, if available, and shards of crisp skin.

There's nothing more Australian than a barbecue, so I was delighted to cook this for Craig Starr and his delightful family who run Gold Creek Station outside Canberra – that is, after I had rounded up sheep, watched one being shorn and driven a tractor!

BARBECUED BEEF SIRLOIN WITH NATIVE FLAVOURS

SERVES 8

PREPARATION
5 minutes

COOKING
50 minutes, plus
10 minutes resting

WINE

The aromatics and pepperiness of these spices cry out for a shiraz or grenache.

LYNDEY'S NOTE

The beef can be browned in a frying pan and then finished in the oven. For 450 g (1 lb) allow 10–15 minutes for medium–rare, 15–20 minutes for medium, 20–25 minutes for medium–well and 25–30 minutes for well done.

2 kg (4 lb 6 oz) beef sirloin (boneless centre cut), removed from the fridge at least 30 minutes prior to cooking
1½ tablespoons ground native pepper
1½ tablespoons sea salt flakes
2 teaspoons ground wattleseed
80 ml (2½ fl oz/⅓ cup) extra-virgin olive oil
2 teaspoons dried lemon myrtle
2 sweet potatoes (about 800 g/1 lb 12 oz in total), peeled and cut into 5 mm (¼ in) slices
eight flat mushrooms (about 600 g/ 1 lb 5 oz in total)
1 bunch thyme, leaves removed

Preheat a barbecue to high.

Score the fat side of the beef in a diamond pattern. Combine the native pepper, salt and wattleseed in a small bowl. Brush the beef with 1 tablespoon of the oil and rub with the spices. Place the beef, fat side down, on the barbecue and cook for 5–7 minutes, or until caramelised. Turn and brown the beef all over for another 5–10 minutes. Reduce the heat and continue to cook as desired, ideally by closing the hood on a covered barbecue. Alternatively, the beef can be finished in a 180°C (350°F) oven for approximately 30 minutes. Turn halfway through. Remove to a plate, cover with foil and rest for at least 10 minutes.

While the beef is resting, combine the remaining oil with the dried lemon myrtle and season with salt. Toss in a bowl with the sweet potato and then cook on the barbecue until tender, turning when browned on one side. Brush the mushrooms with the remaining oil and add to the barbecue. Cook, turning once, until both the sweet potatoes and mushrooms are tender.

To serve, slice the beef thinly and serve with the sweet potato and mushrooms. Scatter with the thyme leaves.

A highlight of my visit to the Wonga Wetlands near Albury was meeting Wiradjuri woman Leonie McIntosh, who has learned the traditional ways from her elders. She showed me a 2000-year-old rock mortar and pestle used to grind native spices like wattleseed. She likes to use these ingredients in a modern way and shared this recipe with me.

WATTLESEED DAMPER

SERVES 6–8

PREPARATION
10 minutes

COOKING
35 minutes

LYNDEY'S NOTE

In order to get a stronger flavour from the wattleseed, infuse it in the milk and water mixture for an hour before use. Leonie recommends serving this with bush tomato butter, made by adding 2 teaspoons ground bush tomato (akudjura) to 250 g (9 oz) soft butter to combine. Leonie says that it adds a savoury flavour to the butter, similar to Vegemite.

300 g (10½ oz/2 cups) self-raising flour
½ teaspoon salt
3 teaspoons wattleseed
30 g (1 oz) butter, diced

125 ml (4 fl oz/½ cup) milk plus
  1 tablespoon extra to glaze
125 ml (4 fl oz/½ cup) water

Preheat the oven to 220°C (430°F) and line a baking tray with baking paper.

Sift the flour and salt into a large bowl, add the wattleseed and mix well. Add the butter and rub in lightly with your fingertips. Combine the milk and water, make a well in the centre of the flour and pour in the liquid all at once. Mix quickly to make a soft dough.

Turn the dough onto a floured surface, knead lightly and form into a 12 cm (4¾ in) round. Place on the baking tray and glaze with the extra milk.

Bake for 15 minutes then reduce the heat to 190°C (375°F). Bake for another 10 minutes, turn the damper over then cook for a further 10 minutes or until the damper sounds hollow when tapped.

To serve, cut into thick wedges and dot with butter and a good dollop of honey, jam or a condiment of your choice.

Variations of Scottish oatmeal biscuits (cookies) were made and sent to soldiers of the Australian and New Zealand Army Corps (ANZAC) in the First World War. However, the Australian War Memorial in Canberra, suggests that they were not named Anzac biscuits until after the war, when they were made and sold as fundraisers for returned soldiers. This recipe is a further evolution by Leonie McIntosh, a Wiradjuri woman from Albury, and incorporates native wattleseed.

WATTLESEED ANZACS

MAKES 25

PREPARATION
10 minutes

COOKING
12 minutes

TO DRINK
A cup of billy tea!

125 g (4½ oz) butter
2 tablespoons golden syrup, dark corn syrup or treacle
1 teaspoon bicarbonate of soda (baking soda)
boiling water
90 g (3 oz/1 cup) rolled (porridge) oats

65 g (2¼ oz/¾ cup) shredded coconut
75 g (2¾ oz/½ cup) plain (all-purpose) flour
220 g (8 oz/1 cup) sugar
100 g (3½ oz/¾ cup) finely chopped macadamia nuts
2 tablespoons wattleseed

Preheat the oven to 180°C (350°F) and line two baking trays with baking paper.

Melt the butter and golden syrup in a saucepan over medium heat. Dissolve the bicarbonate of soda in 2 tablespoons boiling water. Remove the saucepan from the heat and stir through the bicarbonate of soda mixture.

In a large bowl, combine the oats, coconut, flour, sugar, macadamia nuts and wattleseed. Pour over the melted mixture and mix well. Place tablespoons of the mixture onto the prepared trays, allowing room for spreading.

Bake for 10–12 minutes or until light golden brown. Remove from the oven and cool for a few minutes on the tray before removing to a wire rack to cool completely. Store in an airtight container.

Lyndey fly fishing with Ken Helm of Helm Wines in Murrumbateman, outside Canberra.

THE HIGH
COUNTRY

TOP: Thredbo in the majestic Snowy Mountains, New South Wales.

BOTTOM LEFT: Geese at Phillippe Kanyaro's farm outside Tamworth, New South Wales.

BOTTOM RIGHT: Lyndey with Peter and Sally Strelitz and their four children, from Armidale's Milly Hill Lamb farm in New South Wales.

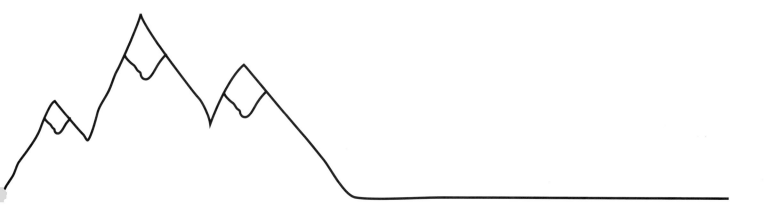

Of all the mountainous regions in Australia, the Great Dividing Range is the most impressive, running down the eastern side of Australia from the Cape York Peninsula in Far North Queensland, 3700 kilometres (2300 miles) south to the Grampians in Victoria. Along its way the Australian Alps have their highest peak, Mount Kosciuszko, 2228 metres (7310 feet) above sea level. This is part of the Snowy Mountains of New South Wales, affectionately known as the Snowies. Here you feel like you're on the top of the world, or at least the roof of Australia. While snow bunnies love the skiing and snowboarding, there's plenty to do when the snow melts. It is a miraculous place to visit in summer, driving through the dramatic landscape with the ghostly snowgums, or the more adventurous bike ride down the mountains. There's something incredibly pure and fresh about the air and the intense flavour it gives the produce.

At Wildbrumby Schnapps Distillery, raspberry schnapps is made from estate-grown raspberries, with bugs kept away by a companion planting of tansy, horseradish and garlic. Brad Spalding was a ski school instructor for many years and he and his Austrian wife, Monika, run an immaculate café complete with distillery on site, as well as making a wide range of schnapps, ideal for the alpine lifestyle.

The area is perhaps best known internationally for the Snowy Mountains hydro-electric scheme, largely built post Second World War by the many migrants who came to Australia. Thirty-seven different nationalities built this great engineering feat. There are plenty of lakes and water courses in the Snowies, but fishing is always a challenge on camera. I was really keen to catch my own Murray cod, as I have long been a fan of this meaty native Australian fish. However, this was not to be, but fishing is not only about catching fish; it's about peacefulness and relaxing in nature.

Sheep roaming the farm at Milly Hill,
award-winning lamb producers in
Armidale, New South Wales.

By contrast, Hobbitt Farm, at 1350 metres (4429 feet), Australia's highest dairy, is all action. The inquisitive goats greet you warmly, trying to jump into cars, eat equipment and generally get in the way. Despite the belief that they are ideally suited to the rocky mountainside, they generally inhabit that terrain as cows get the best land. I found the goats endearing and remarkably fearless and had my first go at milking one by hand before trying a sensational array of goat's cheese.

Wild brumbies are the stuff of myth and legend in Australia, immortalised in poems and films. A brumby is a wild horse and Snowy Mountains brumbies are descended from the horses which came out on the First Fleet and, with cross-breeding, could now be almost anything. I'm always up for a challenge, so at Snowy Wilderness resort I found myself riding one, the first time I'd been in a saddle since I was a teenager. Although owner Justin MacIntosh offered me a five-day ride, I preferred to try out his cooking in a camp oven.

Then I boot scooted my way up to the Northern Tablelands to Tamworth, Armidale and Nundle for Australia Day and, of course, the internationally renowned Tamworth Country Music Festival. Multiculturalism is celebrated in Australia and I was thrilled to cook with Frenchman Phillippe Kanyaro. Not only had he raised the free-range goose we ate, but he built the wood-fired oven we cooked it in, too.

Australia Day on 26 January is always a highlight, because I have been an Australia Day ambassador for over a decade. This is when we celebrate how far we have come as a nation, our people, our land, our diversity, a 'fair go', our different cultures and freedom of speech. No matter how large or small the community, everyone gets into the spirit of the day. Nundle may be one of the area's smaller communities, but it certainly packs a punch when it comes to community spirit.

Tamworth is about celebrating all things country, from camp drafting with the ladies champion Simone Harvey, to learning how to crack a whip or line dance with the locals in the street. The Tamworth Country Music Festival is the biggest in the southern hemisphere and has been wowing both Australian and international guests for an amazing 41 years. It's not only about concerts and big events but music in pubs, clubs and the streets. It was great fun and I caught up with festival old-timer and fiddler, Pixie Jenkins.

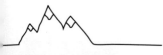

Just over 100 kilometres (62 miles) away, Armidale is home to Peter and Sally Strelitz and their four beautiful children, the people behind the highly acclaimed Milly Hill Lamb. It's all about the quality of the grazing land, the genetics and the feeding regime that produces a consistent end result. There is a growing number of wineries in the area and it's also a university town, the University of New England being the first regional university established in Australia.

The World Heritage listed Blue Mountains is quite a different area. The mountains only range from 200 to 1100 metres (655 to 3610 feet), but are just one and a half hours from Sydney so it's perfect for a quick overnight getaway. The area is as famous for culture as it is for astonishing views. The Norman Lindsay Gallery & Museum in Faulconbridge utilises the talented artist's old home and studio as a gallery to showcase his etchings, drawings, paintings, books and sculptures. The Blue Mountains is also home to historic treasures like the Carrington Hotel (1883) and Everglades Historic House & Gardens. In nearby picturesque Leura, Jodie Van Der Velden weaves her chocolate magic at Josophan's.

However, it is also a region for a surprising range of fresh produce. Autumn is wild mushroom time and further west the eerily quiet Oberon forest is a great location to forage for exotic saffron milk caps (pine mushrooms) and slippery Jack mushrooms. Bella Hyde from FinSki's was a wonderful guide. In partnership with her best friend, Katriina (aka Blondie), they draw on their Finnish and Polish heritages, but like to keep the exact location in the forest secret.

There's even an orchard, Logan Brae Orchard, dating from 1919, which celebrates old apple varieties and ways of working, and with a sensational flavour result. This was only one of the times I got to drive a tractor!

Down in the Megalong Valley Takao Suzuki – who came to Australia 'because he wanted to be a cowboy' – raises and feeds wagyu beef along traditional Japanese lines. The end result is a moist, melt-in-the-mouth, high-quality beef. Above all it is a sense of community which binds this region together.

Blondie and Bella (Katriina and Izabella) from FinSki's, who lead mushroom foraging tours in Oberon, New South Wales, shared this recipe with me. The dough is enriched with butter, a traditional Polish technique.

MUSHROOM AND WALNUT PILLOWS WITH SAFFRON MILK CAP SAUCE

SERVES 4 as an appetiser

PREPARATION
1 hour

COOKING
40 minutes

WINE
The rich flavours of umami (the fifth taste) in these mushrooms sings with chardonnay or cabernet sauvignon or a cabernet blend.

MUSHROOM FILLING
1 tablespoon extra-virgin olive oil
½ brown onion, very finely chopped (use the remaining half for the sauce)
1 garlic clove, finely chopped
250 g (9 oz) saffron milk caps (pine mushrooms) or Swiss brown mushrooms, very finely chopped
1 tablespoon white wine
25 g (1 oz/¼ cup) walnuts, toasted and finely chopped
1 tablespoon saffron milk cap (pine mushroom) or porcini mushroom powder (see Lyndey's note)
salt and freshly ground black pepper

DOUGH
335 g (12 oz/2¼ cups) plain (all-purpose) flour
50 g (1¾ oz) butter, softened
170 ml (5½ fl oz/⅔ cup) water, at room temperature (approximately)

MUSHROOM SAUCE
1 tablespoon extra-virgin olive oil
½ brown onion, very finely chopped
1 tablespoon saffron milk cap (pine mushroom) or porcini mushroom powder (see Lyndey's note)
2 tablespoons white wine
190 ml (6½ fl oz/¾ cup) good-quality chicken stock
190 ml (6½ fl oz/¾ cup) thickened (whipping) cream
flat-leaf (Italian) parsley to garnish

For the mushroom filling, heat the oil in a frying pan over medium heat, add the onion and cook for 5 minutes or until lightly browned. Add the garlic and cook for another 2 minutes. Add the mushrooms and cook for 5 minutes or until all the moisture is absorbed and the mixture is dry. Add the wine, walnuts and mushroom powder and cook for a further 2 minutes. Season to taste with salt and pepper. Remove from the heat and let the mixture cool completely.

For the dough, place the flour in a large bowl, add the butter and, using your fingertips, rub the butter into the flour until the mixture resembles breadcrumbs. Gradually add the water – just enough to bring the dough together. When the dough forms a ball, knead it on a floured surface for 5–10 minutes or until it feels elastic and malleable. Place the dough in a clean bowl, cover and set aside to rest for 15 minutes in the refrigerator.

For the mushroom sauce, heat the oil in a frying pan over medium heat, add the onion and cook for 5 minutes or until softened. Add the mushroom powder and cook for 2 minutes – the mushroom powder will start to give off a beautiful aroma. Add the wine and cook for 2 minutes, then add the chicken stock, bring to a boil and reduce by half. Set aside until ready to use.

To fill the dough, roll out the dough to approximately 2 mm (⅛ in) thick and, using an 8 cm (3¼ in) round cutter, cut out 24 rounds and brush the edge of each round with water. Top with a heaped teaspoon of filling, fold in half to form pillows and gently press the edges together, making sure to squeeze out the air.

Meanwhile, bring a large saucepan of salted water to the boil. Add the cream to the mushroom sauce, place back on the heat and simmer while you cook the pillows.

Cook the pillows in batches in the boiling salted water for 3 minutes or until they float to the surface. Lift out and drain using a slotted spoon and place in the mushroom sauce. Repeat with the remaining pillows.

To serve, place six of the pillows in each bowl and spoon over any remaining mushroom sauce. Garnish with the parsley.

Hobbitt Farm in Jindabyne is the highest dairy in Australia at 1350 metres (4429 feet). The goats were frisky but appealing and I used the chèvre from their milk for this quick and easy recipe

SPICY GOAT'S CHEESE QUESADILLA

MAKES 1

PREPARATION
10 minutes

COOKING
25 minutes

3 garlic cloves, unpeeled
1 jalapeño chilli
4 baby roma (plum), grape or cherry
    tomatoes, halved if large
½ teaspoon cumin seeds
salt and freshly ground black pepper

1 tablespoon extra-virgin olive oil
45 g (1½ oz) prosciutto (about 4 slices)
2 large flour tortillas
100 g (3½ oz) soft goat's cheese
30 g (1 oz/¾ cup) rocket (arugula)

WINE

Goat's cheese is a classic match for sauvignon blanc, with fruity flavours that can handle the heat of the chilli, too.

LYNDEY'S NOTE

To flip the quesadilla more easily, cover the top with a dinner plate and turn out the tortilla, then slide back into the pan.

Place a non-stick frying pan, large enough for one tortilla to lie flat, over medium–high heat. Add the garlic and jalapeño and cook, turning frequently, until softened and blistered. When nearly soft, add the baby roma tomatoes and cook for 2–4 minutes or until softened and blistered. Add the cumin seeds for the last minute and cook until aromatic. Remove from the heat and allow to cool.

Peel the garlic cloves and peel and halve the jalapeño. Place the garlic, jalapeño, tomatoes and cumin seeds, and salt and pepper to taste, into a mortar and use a pestle to pound until smooth.

Heat half the oil in the pan over medium–high heat. Add the prosciutto and cook until crisp, turning if necessary. Remove to a plate.

Brush one flour tortilla with the oil from the pan (or extra oil). Place the tortilla, oil side down, into the clean pan. Taking care not to fill the ingredients right to the edge, spread over the tomato and jalapeño paste then top with slices of crisp prosciutto. Crumble over the goat's cheese, add the rocket leaves and season to taste.

Cover with the second tortilla, pressing to seal. Brush the top of the tortilla with the remaining oil and place over medium–high heat. Cook for 2–3 minutes, pressing down occasionally. Turn carefully and cook for a further 2 minutes, until the cheese is slightly melted and the tortilla is crisp. Cut into eight wedges and serve immediately.

Justin from Snowy Wilderness resort in Jindabyne cooked this for me in a camp oven. Simple, lemony and delicious, it works just as well in a normal oven. Half a hot smoked trout yields about 115 g (4 oz) flesh.

SMOKED TROUT FRITTATA

SERVES 4

PREPARATION
10 minutes

COOKING
15 minutes

WINE

As this makes a lovely breakfast or lunch dish, try a sparkling wine with it!

half a 350 g (12½ oz) hot smoked
   whole trout
12 free-range eggs

juice and grated zest of 1 lemon
60 ml (2 fl oz/¼ cup) extra-virgin olive oil

Preheat the oven to 200°C (400°F).

Remove the skin and bones from the trout and flake it into small pieces.

In a large bowl break the eggs, ensuring no shell gets into the mixture. If a bit of shell does fall in, use half of an egg shell to scoop it out. Add the smoked trout pieces and lemon juice and zest and mix using a fork.

Place a 26–28 cm (10¼–11 in) non-stick ovenproof frying pan over medium heat. Add the oil and tilt the pan to ensure that the oil covers the base and sides of the pan. When hot remove from the heat, pour over the egg and trout mixture and place in the oven. Cook for 15 minutes or until set. If the middle of the frittata 'wobbles,' return it to the oven for a further 5 minutes.

Serve hot, warm or cold sliced into wedges with toast.

While not strictly speaking a tartare, this recipe was created by Monika Spalding from Wildbrumby Schnapps Distillery in Thredbo, using local Snowy Mountains hot smoked trout. One whole trout will yield about 230 g (8 oz) flesh.

SMOKED TROUT 'TARTARE' WITH GRANNY SMITH AND WALNUT SALAD

SERVES 4 as an appetiser

PREPARATION 15 minutes

COOKING 10 minutes

WINE

Much as schnapps would be wonderful here, a riesling or semillon would make a more moderate option.

60 g (2 oz/½ cup) walnut pieces
2 tablespoons caster (superfine) sugar
1 small granny smith apple
1½ tablespoons lemon juice
2 celery stalks, cut into 5 mm (¼ in) matchsticks
1 tablespoon finely chopped dill, plus 4 dill sprigs to serve

1 teaspoon apple cider vinegar
1 tablespoon apple or pear schnapps or apple juice
1 tablespoon extra-virgin olive oil
salt and freshly ground black pepper
1 x 350 g (12½ oz) hot smoked whole trout
1 tablespoon sour cream

Place the walnut pieces in a small non-stick frying pan over medium heat and toss for a few minutes to toast. Sprinkle over the caster sugar, reduce the heat to low and cook for 5 minutes or until caramelised, turning frequently with a silicone spatula. Be careful not to burn the sugar. Remove the nuts from the pan, place on a piece of baking paper and allow to cool.

Peel and core the apple, cut into matchsticks and place in a small bowl. Add the lemon juice, celery, chopped dill, apple cider vinegar, schnapps and oil. Season to taste with salt and pepper.

Remove the skin and bones from the trout, flake into large pieces and divide among four small plates. Top the trout with the dressed apple and celery mixture and caramelised walnuts. Place a teaspoon of sour cream on each plate, top with a dill sprig and serve immediately.

While Murray cod is indigenous to Australia, our great Snowy Mountains hydro-electric scheme was built by migrants, whose participation and cultures have made this country so rich. The 'peperonata' salad is a nod to the Italian heritage that has contributed so much to our culture and food.

MURRAY COD WITH 'PEPERONATA' AND WILTED SPINACH

SERVES 4

PREPARATION
15 minutes

COOKING
10 minutes

WINE

As this is quite a robust dish, go for an Italian varietal like sangiovese. The flavours are quite Spanish too, so a tempranillo could also work well.

LYNDEY'S NOTE

Peperonata is a rustic Italian dish. All the ingredients are gently stewed together and it can be served hot, at room temperature or cold. This version is more like a salad. Grape, cherry or baby roma (plum) tomatoes also make a great addition.

1 tablespoon extra-virgin olive oil
salt and freshly ground black pepper
4 x 175 g (6 oz) Murray cod fillets, skin on
200 g (7 oz) baby English spinach leaves
1 garlic clove, finely chopped

PEPERONATA-STYLE SALAD
1 red capsicum (bell pepper)
1 yellow capsicum (bell pepper)

½ red onion, thinly sliced
1½ tablespoons red wine vinegar
1 tablespoon baby capers, rinsed and drained
50 g (1¾ oz/⅓ cup) black olives, pitted and finely chopped
1½ tablespoons extra-virgin olive oil
salt and freshly ground black pepper
½ bunch basil, cut into very fine shreds

For the peperonata-style salad, chargrill the capsicums over a gas flame, under a grill (broiler) or in the oven until the skins blister and blacken. Place in a plastic bag, seal and set aside to allow the capsicums to steam for 10 minutes. (This makes peeling them much easier.)

Meanwhile, combine the red onion and red wine vinegar in a small bowl. Carefully remove the skin and seeds from the capsicums and slice into 5 mm (¼ in) strips. Combine the capsicum strips, baby capers, black olives, oil and the red onion and red wine vinegar mixture and season to taste with salt and pepper. Lastly top with the basil.

Heat the oil in a large frying pan over medium heat. Pinbone the Murray cod to remove any stray bones. Sprinkle with salt and pepper on the skin side and place, skin side down, in the pan. After a couple of minutes cover the pan and cook until the skin is crisp and the fish is almost cooked through. Remove from the pan and allow to rest to finish off the cooking process. Add the spinach and garlic to the pan used to cook the fish, season with salt and pepper, toss to coat in the oil and wilt.

Place a bed of wilted spinach on each of four serving plates, place the fish, skin side up, on top and spoon some peperonata-style salad on the fish. Serve the remaining salad in a bowl.

Lentils are such a versatile pantry staple. I first developed this recipe to go with salmon, but it's equally good with poultry or meat, or as a vegetarian main course.

MUSTARD LENTILS

SERVES 4 as a side

PREPARATION
10 minutes

COOKING
20 minutes

WINE

Try a lighter style of red wine, like pinot noir, sangiovese or barbera.

150 g (5½ oz/1 cup) French-style lentils
1 tablespoon extra-virgin olive oil
1 carrot, finely diced
1 leek, thinly sliced
1 garlic clove, finely chopped
1 tablespoon finely chopped chives
2 tablespoons flat-leaf (Italian) parsley leaves

1 tablespoon baby capers, rinsed and drained
1 tablespoon dijon mustard
juice of ½ lemon, or to taste
½ teaspoon cayenne pepper
salt and freshly ground black pepper
200 g (7 oz) baby English spinach leaves

Place the lentils in a medium saucepan, cover with water by 5 cm (2 in) and bring to the boil. Reduce the heat and simmer for 10 minutes or until the lentils are tender. Drain.

Heat the oil in a large frying pan to medium, add the carrot and cook for 5 minutes. Add the leek and cook for a further 3 minutes. Add the garlic and cook for an additional minute. Add the drained lentils, chives, parsley, capers, mustard, lemon juice and cayenne pepper and mix well. Season to taste with salt and pepper. Stir through the baby English spinach leaves until just wilted and serve.

Phillippe Kanyaro from Le Pruneau restaurant in Tamworth cooked this for us at his home in his wood-fired oven with produce he had grown. Phillippe has easy access to goose carcasses to make stock, but good-quality chicken consommé will work too, as the stock takes 4 hours to make.

ROAST GOOSE WITH WILD GARLIC AND THYME AND STUFFED POTIRON

SERVES 6

PREPARATION
10 minutes, plus time for goose to come to room temperature

COOKING 1½ hours, plus 4 hours if you want to make your own stock, plus resting

WINE
This is a very rich dish, so a wine with some good tannin grip is needed. Try a full-bodied cabernet sauvignon.

1 goose (about 3.5–4 kg/7 lb 12 oz–8 lb 13 oz)
2 lemons
2 tablespoons salt
1 wild garlic bulb, cloves crushed
1 bunch thyme sprigs
1 bunch fennel fronds
2–3 tablespoons goose fat
green beans, cooked in butter and white wine, to serve (optional)

MIREPOIX
1 celery stalk, roughly chopped
1 large carrot, roughly chopped
1 leek, roughly chopped
1 large brown onion, roughly chopped

STUFFED POTIRON
6 potirons (see Lyndey's note)
460 g (1 lb/2 cups) mashed potato (page 152)

MUSHROOM DUXELLES
40 g (1½ oz) butter
100 g (3½ oz) mushrooms, finely diced

SAUCE
300 ml (10 fl oz) Madeira
500 ml (17 fl oz/2 cups) goose stock (see method) or chicken consommé
100 ml (3½ fl oz) pouring (single/light) cream
salt and freshly ground black pepper
20 g (¾ oz) butter

Preheat a wood-fired oven to hot or a conventional oven to 200°C (400°F).

Remove the goose from the refrigerator to bring it to room temperature.

Combine the mirepoix ingredients and place them in a large roasting dish. Rub the outside of the goose with the juice from the lemons and the salt. Stuff the cavity with the juiced lemon halves, garlic and herbs. Place, breast side down, on top of the mirepoix in the roasting dish. Pour the goose fat over the goose and roast in the oven for 45 minutes or until the breasts are cooked through and the juices run clear when a skewer is inserted.

Remove the legs and breasts from the goose, reserving the breasts and carcass. (The carcass can be used to make stock for the sauce.) Return the legs and thighs to the dish and continue to roast for a further 45 minutes. Remove to a warm place, cover loosely with foil and rest.

Mirepoix is a
mixture of chopped
vegetables used as
a flavour base. A
potiron is the French
name for a vegetable
that is a cross
between a pumpkin
(winter squash) and
a squash.

If you wish to make goose stock, place the goose carcass and mirepoix from the roasting dish in a very large saucepan or stockpot. Cover with water, bring to the boil and skim off any scum that rises to the surface. Turn the heat down and simmer gently for 4 hours, skimming occasionally. Strain the stock and discard the carcass and other solids. You will need 500 ml (17 fl oz/2 cups) for this recipe. Store the remainder in the refrigerator or freezer.

For the potiron, slice a small amount from the bottom of each potiron so that it will sit flat in a roasting dish. Take a slice from the stalk end (reserve for the lid) and, using a spoon, scoop out the inside flesh of each potiron and its lid. Fill each potiron with mashed potato and place the lid on top. Place in a roasting dish and roast for 15–20 minutes.

Meanwhile make the mushroom duxelles by melting the butter over medium heat in a small frying pan. Add the mushrooms and cook gently, stirring occasionally for 5–10 minutes or until soft.

For the sauce, add the madeira to a medium saucepan and place over high heat. Add 500 ml (17 fl oz/2 cups) goose stock or chicken consommé. Boil to reduce by about three-quarters and then whisk in the cream. Season with salt and pepper, turn the heat to low and whisk in the butter until it is melted and the sauce is glossy. Do not boil. Keep warm until ready to serve.

To serve, remove the lid of each potiron, spoon over the mushroom duxelles and replace the lid. Carve the goose by separating the wings from the breasts and legs from the thighs; slice the breast and serve with the beans (if desired), goose and madeira sauce.

I cooked this at Petersons winery in Armidale using some of their stunning wines, after I picked up some award-winning lamb backstrap from Peter and Sally Strelitz from Milly Hill Lamb farm.

POACHED LAMB IN FRESH VINE LEAVES WITH WARM CAULIFLOWER SALAD

SERVES 4

PREPARATION
20 minutes

COOKING
20 minutes

WINE

The joy of this dish is that it is relatively light, so it calls for a lighter style of wine like a pinot noir or, if you are a white wine lover, a chardonnay.

LYNDEY'S NOTE

While I had the treat of using fresh vine leaves, you can use preserved vine leaves. Simply wash them and pat dry with paper towel.

4 fresh vine leaves
1 large red chilli, finely chopped
4 garlic cloves, finely chopped
4 anchovy fillets in oil, drained
1 teaspoon cumin seeds
1 teaspoon fennel seeds
salt and freshly ground black pepper
1 tablespoon extra-virgin olive oil
2 x 300 g (10½ oz) lamb backstraps (loin)
250 ml (8½ fl oz/1 cup) white wine
500 ml (17 fl oz/2 cups) chicken stock

CAULIFLOWER SALAD
1 tablespoon extra-virgin olive oil
50 g (1¾ oz/⅓ cup) pitted kalamata olives, halved
2 tablespoons baby capers, rinsed and drained
750 g (1 lb 11 oz) cauliflower
salt and freshly ground black pepper
125 ml (4 fl oz/½ cup) verjuice (optional)
30 g (1 oz) feta, crumbled
1 tablespoon fresh oregano leaves or flat-leaf (Italian) parsley leaves

Blanch the vine leaves in boiling water for a few minutes. Drain and refresh under cold water. Place on paper towel to remove any excess moisture. Using a mortar and pestle or a small food processor, make a paste with the chilli, garlic, anchovies, cumin and fennel and season to taste with salt and pepper. Add the oil to the paste. Cut each backstrap in half horizontally. Using a sharp knife, make a pocket along the long side of each half ending 2 cm (¾ in) from each end. Season inside the pockets and on the outside generously. Spoon the paste into the pockets and wrap a vine leaf around the middle to cover the pocket. Secure the vine leaf around the lamb with kitchen string. Place the wine and stock in a saucepan or frying pan large enough to hold the lamb in a single layer. Top up with extra water if necessary and bring to the boil. Lower the heat to a simmer and add the lamb parcels. Poach the lamb gently for 6 minutes, turning over once halfway through cooking. Remove from the heat and allow to rest in the poaching liquid for 5–10 minutes.

Meanwhile, prepare the cauliflower salad by heating the oil in a large frying pan over medium–high heat. Add the olives and capers and fry for 2 minutes. Slice the cauliflower into large slices about 1 cm (½ in) thick. Add to the pan and season. Cook, tossing occasionally, for 5 minutes or until golden and slightly softened. When almost cooked, add the verjuice, if using, and reduce for a minute or two. To serve, divide the cauliflower salad among four plates and top with the crumbled feta and oregano leaves. Remove the string from the lamb, cut each piece in half diagonally and serve beside the salad.

A pork shoulder is the usual cut choice for pulled pork. However, it can take three or more hours to cook. My method uses pork scotch steaks, which are slices of pork neck. Cooked this way the pork is just as delicious, with a guarantee that tangy, spicy shreds of melt-in-your-mouth pork will be ready to eat in just over an hour. I cooked this in front of the fire at the Carrington Hotel, Katoomba in the Blue Mountains.

EASY PULLED PORK WITH APPLE AND BRUSSELS SPROUTS SLAW

SERVES 4

PREPARATION
15 minutes

COOKING 1¼ hours

WINE
The spice in this dish calls for a peppery shiraz from a cool climate, or even a tempranillo.

1 tablespoon ground cumin
2 teaspoons ground coriander
2 teaspoons smoked paprika
1 teaspoon dried red chilli flakes
1 teaspoon mustard powder
½ teaspoon sea salt flakes
3 garlic cloves, finely chopped
4 pork scotch or neck steaks (about 700 g/1 lb 9 oz in total)
2 tablespoons extra-virgin olive oil
1 red onion, thinly sliced
500 ml (17 fl oz/2 cups) chicken stock
60 ml (2 fl oz/¼ cup) apple cider vinegar
1 tablespoon brown sugar

4 thick slices sourdough bread or rolls to serve
½ cup coriander (cilantro) leaves (optional)

APPLE AND BRUSSELS SPROUTS SLAW
1 apple, quartered and cored
1 small fennel bulb, trimmed and fronds reserved
210 g (7½ oz) brussels sprouts (about 7), blanched, refreshed and leaves separated
2 spring onions (scallions), thinly sliced
2 tablespoons lemon juice
60 ml (2 fl oz/¼ cup) extra-virgin olive oil
salt and freshly ground black pepper

Combine the cumin, ground coriander, paprika, chilli flakes, mustard powder, salt and garlic in a shallow bowl. Press both sides of each pork steak into the spice mixture.

Heat the oil in a large flameproof casserole dish over medium heat then cook the pork steaks with the remaining spice mixture for 2 minutes on each side until browned. Add the sliced onion, stock, apple cider vinegar and brown sugar and bring to the boil. Cover, reduce the heat and simmer for 1 hour or until the pork is very tender. Carefully remove the pork steaks from the liquid and set aside. Bring the remaining liquid to the boil over medium heat and simmer for 10 minutes or until thickened.

Shred the pork using two forks, add to the reduced sauce and stir gently, being careful not to break up the meat further.

For the apple and brussels sprouts slaw, shred the apple and fennel using a sharp knife or mandoline and place in a bowl. Add the reserved fennel fronds, brussels sprouts leaves, spring onions, lemon juice, oil and season to taste with salt and pepper.

To serve, spoon the pulled pork onto the bread, top with the slaw and scatter over the coriander leaves, if using.

Wagyu is heavily marbled beef and is best served thinly sliced and quickly cooked to render the fat. Who would believe that it is traditionally farmed in the Blue Mountains. Everglades Historic House & Gardens made a stunning setting for me to cook this dish.

SEARED WAGYU WITH MUSHROOM RAGU AND ZUCCHINI SALAD

SERVES 4

PREPARATION 10 minutes

COOKING 15 minutes

WINE

A minty cabernet sauvignon will go well with both the zucchini salad and the mushrooms and has enough tannin to stand up to the rich flavour of the wagyu.

LYNDEY'S NOTE

Saffron milk cap mushrooms can carry a lot of dirt. To clean, wipe with a damp cloth or brush with a pastry brush.

4 x 180 g (6½ oz) wagyu steaks
salt and freshly ground black pepper
1 tablespoon extra-virgin olive oil
¼ cup mint leaves, torn

MUSHROOM RAGU

30 g (1 oz) butter
100 g (3½ oz) saffron milk cap (pine) mushrooms or Swiss brown or portobello mushrooms, cleaned
4 thyme sprigs
80 ml (2½ fl oz/⅓ cup) chicken stock
salt and freshly ground black pepper

ZUCCHINI SALAD

2 zucchini (courgettes)
grated zest and juice of 1 lemon
60 ml (2 fl oz/¼ cup) extra-virgin olive oil
1 garlic clove, finely chopped
1 large red chilli, seeded and finely chopped
salt and freshly ground black pepper

For the mushroom ragu, melt the butter in a medium frying pan over medium heat until it starts to foam. Add the saffron milk cap mushrooms (torn in half if large) and cook for a minute or so. Add the thyme sprigs, chicken stock and season to taste with salt and pepper. Cook for 7–8 minutes, stirring occasionally, until the mushrooms are soft and the stock has evaporated.

For the zucchini salad, using a vegetable peeler or sharp knife, shave the zucchini into thin strips. Combine the lemon zest and juice, oil, garlic and chilli in a bowl and whisk. Season to taste with salt and pepper.

To cook the wagyu, heat a frying pan over medium heat. Season the steaks with salt and pepper. Add the oil to the frying pan and, after 30 seconds, add the steaks. Cook for 1–2 minutes on each side or until cooked as desired. Remove and rest in a warm place for 5 minutes.

To serve, pour the dressing over the zucchini and toss gently to combine then top with the torn mint leaves. Serve with the wagyu and mushroom ragu.

When I cooked in the beautiful grounds of Petersons winery in Armidale, I was told these beef cheeks from chef Melissa Darmanin are one of her most popular dishes. While she likes to use tomato paste (concentrated tomato purée), I find tomato passata (puréed tomatoes) gives a lighter end product.

RED AND WHITE WINE BRAISED BEEF CHEEKS

SERVES 4

PREPARATION
20 minutes

COOKING 6 hours
25 minutes

WINE

A big powerful dish like this needs a big powerful wine, so try shiraz, durif or zinfandel.

1 tablespoon extra-virgin olive oil
salt and freshly ground black pepper
4 beef cheeks (about 800 g–1 kg/
   1 lb 12 oz–2 lb 3 oz in total) trimmed
   of all fat and sinew
1 small brown onion, finely chopped
3 garlic cloves, finely chopped
2 small carrots, cut into 1 cm (½ in) dice
1½ celery stalks, cut into 1 cm (½ in) dice
2 small bay leaves
3 thyme sprigs
100 g (3½ oz) button mushrooms

160 ml (5½ fl oz) tomato passata
   (puréed tomatoes)
310 ml (10½ fl oz/1¼ cups) red wine
310 ml (10½ fl oz/1¼ cups) white wine
190 ml (6½ fl oz/¾ cup) good-quality
   beef stock
125 g (4½ oz) cherry tomatoes
1 tablespoon brown sugar
¼ bunch flat-leaf (Italian) parsley
40 g (1½ oz/½ cup) freshly grated
   parmesan (optional)

Preheat the oven to 150°C (300°F).

Place the oil in a flameproof casserole dish or heavy-based ovenproof pan over high heat until it begins to smoke. Place the seasoned beef cheeks in to brown and seal, approximately 30–40 seconds each side. Remove and set aside. Reduce the heat to low, add the onion and cook for 5–10 minutes or until soft and translucent. Add the garlic and cook for a further 2 minutes. Turn the heat to medium and add the carrots, celery, bay leaves, thyme sprigs and button mushrooms and cook for a further 2 minutes.

Add the tomato passata, red and white wine and stock. Stir well and reduce the heat to very low. Add the beef cheeks with any juice to the casserole, arranging evenly and making sure the cheeks are covered with the sauce. Grind some black pepper in but do not season with salt until the end.

Place the lid on the casserole and cook in the oven for 5–6 hours, checking each hour. If necessary, splash with a little extra liquid. In the last hour of cooking add the cherry tomatoes and the brown sugar. Stir through the chopped parsley just before serving.

The beef cheeks are ready when they fall apart when cut with a butter knife. The sauce should be thickened, not watery. If not, remove the beef cheeks to a warm place, put the dish on top of the stove and boil to reduce and thicken the sauce. Taste and adjust the seasoning if necessary.

Serve the beef cheeks with mashed potato (page 152), or a garlic and chive mash with lots of grated parmesan, if using, over the top.

It was wonderful to stay at the historic Carrington Hotel in Katoomba. The chef Sam Commins shared this gorgeous recipe with me.

GINGER PANNA COTTA WITH APPLE JELLY

SERVES 4

PREPARATION
20 minutes,
plus 1 hour chilling

COOKING
5–10 minutes

WINE

Any botrytised wine would go well here – increasingly we see them made from grape varieties apart from semillon.

10 cm (4 in) piece fresh ginger, peeled
1½ gelatine leaves
300 ml (10 fl oz) thickened (whipping) cream
55 g (2 oz/¼ cup) caster (superfine) sugar

APPLE JELLY
1½ gelatine leaves
190 ml (6½ fl oz/¾ cup) clear apple juice
½ pink lady apple, cored and cut into 5 mm (¼ in) dice

Make some ginger juice by processing the ginger in a food processor with 1 tablespoon water until very finely chopped. Press through a sieve to extract the juice. This should make 60 ml (2 fl oz/¼ cup) ginger juice. Reserve.

Place the gelatine leaves in a bowl, cover with cold water and set aside for 5 minutes or until soft. Drain well.

Meanwhile, place the cream and ginger juice in a small saucepan over medium heat and bring to a simmer. Remove from the heat, add the sugar and stir until it dissolves. Drain and squeeze out the softened gelatine and mix through. Cool to around 60°C (140°F), about 10 minutes. Pour into four dessert glasses and refrigerate for 30 minutes.

While the panna cotta is chilling, prepare the apple jelly. Place the gelatine leaves in a bowl, cover with cold water and set aside for 5 minutes or until soft.

Heat the apple juice in a small saucepan over medium–low heat, to just above blood temperature (45°C/113°F), for about 3 minutes. Remove from the heat. Drain and squeeze out the gelatine, stir it through the apple juice and allow to cool.

Once the panna cotta is set, sprinkle with the diced apple and carefully pour over the apple jelly. Refrigerate for 30 minutes or until set. Serve immediately.

Deconstructed desserts are very popular in restaurants. This one is inspired by peach melba, the dessert developed to celebrate famous Australian opera singer, Dame Nellie Melba.

DECONSTRUCTED PEACH MELBA

SERVES 4

PREPARATION
20 minutes

COOKING
20 minutes

WINE

This is not overly sweet, so try a late-picked riesling.

LYNDEY'S NOTE

A cartouche is a circular round cut from baking paper, just large enough to cover the pan. The cartouche will help the top of the peaches stay submerged and cook evenly.

55 g (2 oz/¼ cup) caster (superfine) sugar
1 strip lemon zest (use juice in sauce)
4 small peaches
4 thyme sprigs
100 g (3½ oz) crème fraîche or light
   sour cream
extra thyme sprigs with flowers to serve
125 g (4½ oz) raspberries to serve

COCONUT AND ALMOND CRUMBLE
45 g (1½ oz/½ cup) flaked almonds
40 g (1½ oz/½ cup) shredded coconut
30 g (1 oz) butter
55 g (2 oz/¼ cup) caster (superfine) sugar
25 g (1 oz/¼ cup) ground almonds

RASPBERRY SAUCE
125 g (4½ oz) raspberries
2 tablespoons icing (confectioners') sugar
juice of ½ lemon

Place water to cover the peaches in a saucepan large enough to hold the fruit in one layer, and bring to the boil with the caster sugar, stirring to dissolve the sugar. Add the lemon zest, peaches and thyme sprigs, reduce the heat and simmer for 10 minutes covered with a cartouche (see Lyndey's note) or until the peaches are just tender. Remove the peaches from the liquid and set aside to cool before peeling, halving and removing the stones. Slice each half into quarters and then into four wedges, or cut into random shapes if you prefer.

For the coconut and almond crumble, toss the flaked almonds in a small frying pan over low heat for 3 minutes or until just starting to colour. Add the coconut and continue to toss for a further 2 minutes or until the flaked almonds and coconut are a light golden colour. Remove to a small bowl. In the same frying pan, add the butter, sugar and ground almonds and cook for 4 minutes until the butter melts and the mixture colours slightly. Remove from the heat and stir through the almonds and coconut then set aside to cool.

For the raspberry sauce, place the raspberries, icing sugar, lemon juice and 2 tablespoons water in a small saucepan. Bring to the boil over high heat, mashing the raspberries to a purée. Reduce the heat and simmer for 1 minute. Push through a sieve to remove the seeds.

To serve, sprinkle each of four plates with the coconut and almond crumble. Top with the peach wedges and teaspoon-sized dollops of crème fraîche. Drizzle over some raspberry sauce, dot with whole raspberries, scatter over the thyme flowers and serve immediately.

Norman Lindsay (1879–1969), artist, cartoonist and writer, was both proficient and prolific in pen and ink drawing, etching, woodcuts, watercolours and sculpture. Lindsay's The Magic Pudding *(1918) is an enduring children's classic so, in the beautiful grounds of the Norman Lindsay Gallery & Museum in Faulconbridge, New South Wales, I cooked my own pudding, using fresh ginger rather than ground ginger to give it a modern edge.*

STEAMED BANANA AND GINGER PUDDING WITH BRÛLÉED BANANAS

SERVES 8

PREPARATION
10 minutes

COOKING
1 hour 25 minutes,
plus 5 minutes
standing time

WINE
The sweet flavours
demand a sweet
wine, so try a late-
picked riesling, or
any 'sticky' wine.

90 g (3 oz) butter, plus extra to grease
115 g (4 oz/⅓ cup) golden syrup, dark corn syrup or treacle
¾ teaspoon bicarbonate of soda (baking soda)
1 ripe banana, mashed, plus 2 bananas, extra, sliced into 1 cm (½ in) pieces diagonally
1 teaspoon grated fresh ginger
60 ml (2 fl oz/¼ cup) milk
125 ml (4 fl oz/½ cup) strong espresso coffee

1 egg
225 g (8 oz/1½ cups) self-raising flour
1½ tablespoons sugar
cream to serve

COFFEE AND GINGER GLAZE
175 g (6 oz/½ cup) golden syrup, dark corn syrup or treacle
45 g (1½ oz) butter
125 ml (4 fl oz/½ cup) strong espresso coffee
½ teaspoon grated fresh ginger

Grease a 2 litre (68 fl oz/8 cup) pudding steamer or heatproof ceramic bowl with butter.

Combine the golden syrup and butter in a medium saucepan and stir over low heat until smooth. Remove from the heat and stir in the bicarbonate of soda.

Whisk the banana, grated ginger, milk, coffee and egg together in a pitcher. Mix the banana mixture and the self-raising flour into the saucepan in two batches and stir until well combined.

Pour the mixture into the prepared steamer or bowl. If using a bowl, cover securely with pleated baking paper and foil. If using a steamer, secure with a lid.

»»»

Place the pudding steamer in a large saucepan with enough boiling water to come halfway up the sides of the steamer; cover the saucepan with a tight-fitting lid. Boil for 75–80 minutes, replenishing the water as necessary to maintain the same level. Stand the pudding for 5 minutes before turning onto a plate.

To make the coffee and ginger glaze, combine all the ingredients in a small saucepan over medium heat, stirring until smooth. Bring to the boil. Reduce the heat and simmer, uncovered, for 2 minutes. Alternatively, combine the ingredients in a microwave-safe pitcher and cook at Medium power for 4 minutes then whisk well.

To brûlée the bananas, sprinkle the sugar over the banana slices. Use a blowtorch to melt the sugar to form a crisp top. Serve the pudding with the glaze, brûléed bananas and cream.

OPPOSITE: The vines at Petersons Winery in Armidale, New South Wales.

PAGES 214–15: Lyndey on Queanbeyan railway station, near Canberra.

Logan Brae is a wonderful old apple orchard at Blackheath, the last one in the Blue Mountains. The lovely cook there, Julia, shared her muffin recipe with me.

APPLE AND BLACKBERRY CRUMBLE MUFFINS

MAKES 8

PREPARATION
25 minutes

COOKING
25 minutes

TO DRINK
Surely some apple juice or a cup of tea or coffee!

225 g (8 oz/1½ cups) plain (all-purpose) flour
165 g (6 oz/¾ cup) sugar
½ teaspoon salt
2 teaspoons baking powder
80 ml (2½ fl oz/⅓ cup) milk
80 ml (2½ fl oz/⅓ cup) vegetable oil
1 egg
1 large granny smith apple
115 g (4 oz/¾ cup) blackberries

CRUMBLE
75 g (2¾ oz/½ cup) plain (all-purpose) flour
60 g (2 oz) butter, chilled and cut into 1 cm (½ in) dice
2 tablespoons caster (superfine) or brown sugar
2 tablespoons slivered almonds, roughly chopped

Preheat the oven to 180°C (350°F). Line eight 125 ml (4 fl oz/½ cup) holes of a muffin tin with paper liners or use disposable baking cups.

For the crumble, place the flour in a small bowl. Add the butter and rub in, using your fingertips, until the mixture resembles breadcrumbs. Stir through the sugar and almonds.

For the muffin mix, combine the flour, sugar, salt and baking powder in a large bowl. In a small bowl or pitcher, whisk the milk, oil and egg until smooth.

Peel and core the apple. Cut half into 1 cm (½ in) dice and grate the remainder.

Add the milk mixture to the dry ingredients with the grated apple, apple dice and blackberries. Mix until just combined.

Spoon into the prepared muffin tin or disposable baking cups, sprinkle with the crumble and bake for 25 minutes or until cooked when tested with a skewer. Serve.

The Pink Lady Apple Liqueur Schnapps from Wildbrumby Schnapps Distillery, halfway between Jindaybyne and Thredbo, was so delicious that I simply had to cook up this lovely cake to use it in and eat with it!

PINK LADY APPLE AND COCONUT CAKE

SERVES 8

PREPARATION
10 minutes

COOKING
30 minutes

WINE
Any sticky wine or a cup of tea or coffee!

LYNDEY'S NOTE
Leaving the skin on the apples helps them hold their shape and adds a lovely texture to the filling.

170 g (6 oz/¾ cup) caster (superfine) sugar
2 teaspoons grated lemon zest
175 g (6 oz) butter, softened
150 g (5½ oz/1 cup) self-raising flour
1½ teaspoons baking powder
pinch of salt
3 eggs
1 teaspoon vanilla bean paste
40 g (1½ oz/½ cup) shredded coconut
2 tablespoons coconut cream

180 g (6½ oz) crème fraîche or light sour cream
icing (confectioners') sugar to dust (optional)

APPLE FILLING
40 g (1½ oz) butter
2 large pink lady apples (about 400 g/ 14 oz in total), cored and thinly sliced
3–4 tablespoons brown sugar to taste
80 ml (2½ fl oz/⅓ cup) pink lady apple schnapps or other apple or pear liqueur

Preheat the oven to 180°C (350°F). Line the bases and grease and flour the sides of two 19 cm (7½ in) cake tins.

Place the sugar and lemon zest in a food processor and pulse to combine. Add the butter, flour, baking powder, salt, eggs and vanilla bean paste and process for 1–2 minutes or until smooth. Add the coconut and coconut cream and pulse until just combined.

Divide the mixture between the tins. Bake in the oven for 30 minutes or until golden and the tops spring back when pressed. Leave the cakes in the tins for 5 minutes to cool slightly and then turn out onto wire racks to cool completely.

Meanwhile for the apple filling, melt the butter in a medium non-stick frying pan over medium–high heat. Add the apples, sprinkle over the brown sugar and cook, turning frequently, until golden and caramelised. Stir through the schnapps and flambé by tilting the pan or lighting it with a match, if desired. Cook until all the liquid has evaporated. Remove from the heat and set aside to cool.

To serve, flip one of the cake layers upside down so the flat side is facing up. Spread over the crème fraîche and top with the apples. Sandwich with the second cake layer. Dust with icing sugar, if desired.

Jodie Van Der Velden from Josophan's Fine Chocolates in Leura explains, 'These delicious little pavé (French for 'cobblestones') are a perfectly simple bite-sized treat. The pavé can be individually dipped in tempered chocolate after the ganache has set and they're cut, or they're also delicious as ganache cubes rolled in high-quality cocoa powder, like Callebaut that contains almost 25 per cent cocoa butter.'

FRESH MINT-INFUSED CHOCOLATE PAVÉ

MAKES about 40

PREPARATION
15 minutes, plus overnight setting

COOKING
10 minutes, plus 45 minutes infusing

WINE

The rich intensity of chocolate demands a fortified wine like a liqueur muscat or topaque.

LYNDEY'S NOTE

To get the pavé texture right, use couverture chocolate. The higher cocoa butter content enables the pavé to set and become firm. If you can't get any, use regular dark chocolate, but reduce the thickened cream to 200 ml (7 fl oz).

1 bunch mint
300 ml (10 fl oz) thickened (whipping) cream

400 g (14 oz) dark couverture chocolate, roughly chopped
good-quality cocoa powder or tempered chocolate to serve

Remove the thick stalks from the base of the mint leaves, and break apart the leaves by twisting and tearing with your hands, to bruise the leaves and release the oil from the mint.

Bring the cream to the boil in a saucepan over high heat. Once it is boiling, drop the torn mint leaves in, remove from the heat and set aside for the mint to infuse for approximately 45 minutes.

Strain the cream by passing it through a sieve, pushing down on the leaves with a spatula to extract as much cream as possible. Discard the leaves.

Return the strained cream to a saucepan over high heat and bring to the boil. Place the chocolate in a heatproof bowl. When the cream is boiling, remove from the heat and pass it through a sieve onto the chocolate. Whisk gently until the chocolate is melted and the mixture is smooth. (Microwave on High in 5-second bursts if not fully melted.)

Pour the mixture into a shallow baking tin (30 cm x 20 cm/12 in x 8 in) lined with baking paper. The ganache will be approximately 1.5 cm (½ in) high. Smooth with a spatula.

Cover with plastic wrap, pressing it onto the surface of the ganache to avoid air pockets, as condensation will spoil the ganache. Set aside overnight to set at room temperature.

The next day, cut into small squares and roll in sifted cocoa powder or dip in tempered chocolate. (If not dipping in chocolate, refrigerate in a sealed container, but serve at room temperature.)

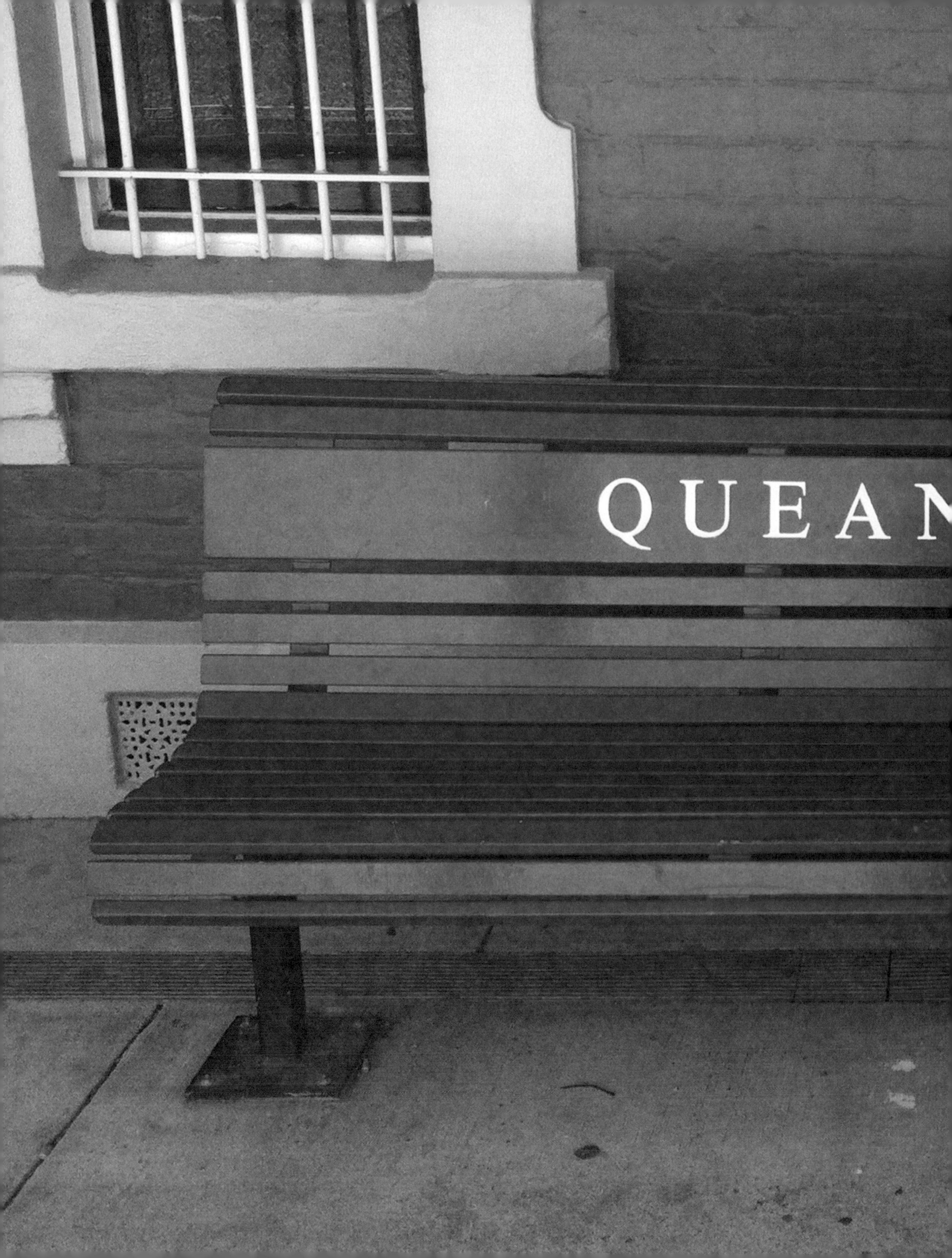
QUEAN

INDEX

Numbers in italics indicate illustrations

ACKNOWLEDGEMENTS

Any book or TV series is a huge collaborative effort and thanks are due to so many. The TV series came first, so first and foremost thanks to my partner in life and business, John Caldon, for your unwavering love and support – without your commitment there would have been no *Taste of Australia*. The TV series was some 18 months in the making from conception to delivery, so thanks to Astrid Sampson, our Head of Production at Flame Media, for keeping us going and sharing the dream; to the cameramen and those who took still photos along the way (Luke Adams, Giovanni Pacialeo, Tom Law, Matt Tiller and Murray Vanderveer); and to the rest of the crew who travelled across this great land, working all hours in all temperatures to create some great television; and to those who worked in post production. Thanks also to the wonderful food and wine producers of Australia who shared their stories, and our partners who came on the journey with us.

For the book itself, thanks to Ann Kidd for her tireless help testing recipes, attending shoots and her eagle eye in proofreading this great tome; to my PAs who helped with recipe testing: Julia Campbell and Rosemary Miller (who also did her share of proofreading); to stylist Georgie Dolling for her incredible eye; and to Stuart Scott for his lovely photos. Thanks also to Sue Williams and Katie Birchall for their help with food photography, and for the following people who supplied props: Country Road, Lisette Martin Designs, Porter's Paints and Prop Co-op, Sydney. Finally, thanks to Paul McNally and all at Hardie Grant for your enthusiasm for this project, and especially to Ariana Klepac for her editing prowess.

For my daughter, Lucy, and her Toby.
A reminder of all that is great about our Australia.

Published in 2014 by Hardie Grant Books

Hardie Grant Books (Australia)
Ground Floor, Building 1
658 Church Street
Richmond, Victoria 3121
www.hardiegrant.com.au

Hardie Grant Books (UK)
Dudley House, North Suite
34–35 Southampton Street
London WC2E 7HF
www.hardiegrant.co.uk

Text © Lyndey Milan
Photography © Stuart Scott
Design © Hardie Grant Books 2014

A Cataloguing-in-Publication entry is available from the catalogue of the
National Library of Australia at www.nla.gov.au
Lyndey Milan's Taste of Australia
ISBN 978 1 7427 0784 6

Publishing director: Paul McNally
Project editors: Hannah Koelmeyer and Meelee Soorkia
Editor: Ariana Klepac
Concept designer: Tania Gomes
Cover designer: Mark Campbell
Designer: Susanne Geppert
Photographer: Stuart Scott
Stylist: Georgina Dolling
Production Manager: Todd Rechner

Colour reproduction by Splitting Image Colour Studio
Printed and bound in China by 1010 Printing International Limited

Find this book on **Cooked.**
www.cooked.com.au
www.cooked.co.uk